An Illustrated Manual

of Traditional

Techniques

THE
TAPESTRY
HANDBOOK

Carol K. Russell

Dedication

The Tapestry Handbook is dedicated
to the 20th-century tapestry weavers
named within.

Published in 1990 by Lark Books
50 College Street
Asheville, North Carolina, U.S.A., 28801

Copyright © 1990, Carol K. Russell

Editor: Carol Taylor
Design: Rob Pulleyn and Thom Boswell
Typesetting: Elaine Thompson
Production: Thom Boswell
Photography (unless otherwise noted):
  George Mauro

ISBN 0-937274-54-2

Library of Congress Cataloging-in-
Publication Data

Russell, Carol K.
    The tapestry handbook / by
      Carol K. Russell
    Includes bibliographical references
      (p. 174)
    ISBN 0-937274-54-2: $24.95
    1. Tapestry. 2. Hand weaving. I. Title

TT849.R87   1990
746.3--dc20   90-31992
                                CIP

Printed in Hong Kong

Acknowledgements

The author would like to acknowledge the expertise and generosity of those who have participated in the realization of this ten-year-long dream. First of all, the artists/weavers responsible for the contemporary tapestries throughout the book have my deepest gratitude—not only for submitting an extraordinarily beautiful and diverse collection of slides, but also for sharing essential technical specifics, insightful personal theories, and, in many cases, bits of their lives as tapestry weavers. Tapestry students now, and for many years to come, will be encouraged and inspired by these eloquent 20th-century expressions.

I must also thank Lise DeCoursin for testing the clarity of the instructional text and for cheerfully and patiently weaving flawless technical illustrations. And Nina Krooss, a talented writer much admired by this fledgling author, who sensitively demonstrated that craftsmanship in writing is as essential as craftsmanship in weaving.

For their gracious assistance acquiring illustrations for the book, I am indebted to Jason Nazmiyal, Suzanne Barner, Carol and Ken Hopper, Diana Gast, and the staff of the Textile Museum.

My wonderful family deserves to be commended: for responding when I was in need of help, and for recognizing when to stay out of my way.

I honor the distinguished professional staff involved with this project: George Mauro, for his obvious photographic genius and his gentle coaching of the author in areas outside her usual realm; editor Carol Taylor, for her wisdom, diplomacy, enviable energy, and amazing organization; the production staff at Lark Books for skillfully attending to every tiny (but crucial) detail; and, ultimately, publisher Rob Pulleyn, for courageously providing the scope for developing this complicated concept according to my own vision.

The following sources have been briefly quoted: Josef Albers, *Interaction of Color*, Yale University Press, 1963; Jean Leymarie, *Picasso: The Artist of the Century*, The Viking Press, 1966; Theo Moorman, *Weaving as an Art Form*, Van Nostrand Reinhold, 1975; Anni Albers, *On Weaving*, Wesleyan University Press, 1965; Anni Albers, *On Designing*, Wesleyan University Press, 1943; "Sculpture's Queen Bee" (Louise Nevelson), *Time*, January 12, 1981; Archie Brennan, in catalogue for the exhibit "Tapestry: The Narrative Voice," 1989-1991; Barbara Rose, *Frankenthaler*, Harry Abrams, 1972; Maitland Graves, *The Art of Color and Design*, McGraw Hill, 1951; Johannes Itten, *The Elements of Color*, Van Nostrand Reinhold, 1970; Dr. Susan H. Auth, curator of the classical collection, the Newark Museum, the exhibit guide "Coptic Art of Ancient Egypt: Treasures From the Nadler Collection and the Newark Museum," May 30 - Nov. 30, 1986; Steve Getzwiller, *The Fine Art of Navajo Weaving*, Ray Manley Publications, 1984; Johann Wolfgang von Goethe, *Theory of Colours*, trans. Charles Lock Eastlake, M.I.T. Press, 1970. "The Red Wheelbarrow" is reprinted from William Carlos Williams, *Collected Poems: Volume I, 1909-1939*, copyright 1938 New Directions Publishing Corporation, by permission of the publisher.

1

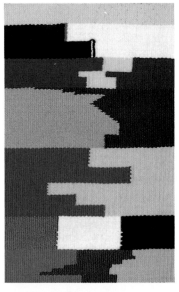

2

Contents

3

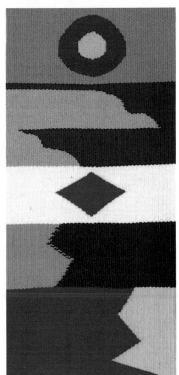

4

5

6

7

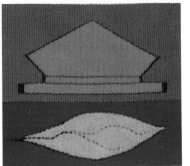

8

Introduction

Having decided to write a book about tapestry techniques, I set out in search of an eclectic array of twentieth-century tapestries that would illustrate the instructional text and place the art of tapestry weaving within a broad contemporary context. My odyssey began on a quiet New England island, where I found a talented tapestry weaver interpreting the extraordinary visual harmonies of the fragile environment near the sea. From Ireland, a weaver contributed compelling images of her personal spiritual insights. In an envelope postmarked Sao Paulo, I received a slide of a sad Brazilian Indian helplessly observing the obscene exploitation of his native land. By way of a tapestry weaver from Canada, I was privileged to share a sensitive portrayal of the devastation of Jewish communities in Prague during the Holocaust.

Inspired by a diversity of places, people, and concepts, the artists represented in this book—and many others throughout the world—eloquently express their individual messages through the universally recognized language of tapestry. Defined technically, tapestry is the interweaving of discontinuous weft yarns with tensioned warp yarns through two alternate sheds, resulting in a firm, weft-surface textile constructed concurrently with the description of its design. Taken as a whole, this definition identifies tapestry's distinctive elements:

1. "discontinuous weft yarns": In most hand-weaving techniques, a weft yarn is passed continuously across each row of weaving. Since the direction of the weft is reversed only at a selvedge (an outside edge), weft colors are interchanged vertically. By contrast, tapestry technique involves several wefts in each row of weaving. Because they can be entered, deleted, or reversed at any point in the row, color can be shifted horizontally.

2. "two alternate sheds": Tapestry weave is the simplest of all woven structures, universally referred to as "tabby" or "plain weave"—that is, each weft is woven over and under successive warps, in opposite order to the weft preceding it.

3. "weft surface textile": Horizontal rows of tightly woven weft completely cover the vertical warps and thus form the surface of the textile.

4. "constructed concurrently with the description of its design": In most visual arts (painting, for instance), the artist adds an image to an existing surface (in this case, a canvas). In tapestry, however, the artist constructs the image and the surface at the same time. This last criterion helps differentiate tapestry from other types of textiles. Embroidery stitched onto a woven surface may be fiber art, but it cannot correctly be defined as tapestry; it does not form the essential structure of the textile.

Within this definition fall centuries of woven works. From fourth-century Egypt come extraordinary Coptic tapestries, whose charming images of people and animals tell us a great deal about the tumultuous times in which they were woven, sometimes combining Christian and pagan iconography. French tapestries range from the magnificent scenes of the Angers Apocalypse to the dazzling contemporary designs of Jean Lurcat. To add to these riches, Indian cultures of North and South America have endowed us with blankets, hangings, and rugs that reflect the unique color and design influences of their culures.

The archives are rich with tapestry-woven textiles from nearly every emerging culture throughout the ages. Using materials painstakingly prepared by hand and the most rudimentary looms, weavers have created culturally expressive and, in many cases, socially profound tapestries. The simple, enduring technique of these treasures will continue to prevail, connecting contemporary tapestry weavers to the past as well as to the future.

It was this connection with other cultures and other times that first compelled me to study tapestry weaving. I learned from excellent teachers and professional weavers, most of whom taught methods firmly rooted in centuries of tradition. I immediately developed a strong affinity for the handsome, heavy structure of tapestry, its technical precision, its sensuous materials, and its almost limitless potential for personal expression.

But even as we diligently mastered and refined the lessons of our ancestors, barriers were being broken down and the parameters of tapestry were being expanded. In the 1960s and '70s, museum and gallery "tapestry" exhibits juxtaposed traditional, flat-woven tapestries with fiber art of unrelated categories, such as macramé or fiber collage. Because it was not sufficiently "different," traditional tapestry weaving began to fall from grace. It was no longer considered special, and many established fiber artists initiated a trend away from all forms of labor-intensive weaving.

Having survived this cycle of unfocused fiber explosions, I am delighted to sense the stirrings of a new trend, a trend toward greater individuality of expression within the characteristic techniques of traditional tapestry. Contemporary designer/weavers seem to take enormous pride in being called "tapestry weavers." They take great care to include in their tapestries only the finest, archival-quality materials. Their designs reflect insights so highly personal that many tapestry weavers have chosen to work on a scale permitting their direct involvement with the execution of every element, reflecting a most welcome freshness, spontaneity, and integration of image and technique. Rather than anonymously reproducing other works of art, the new generation of tapestry weavers strives to develop a distinctive, stylistically unified body of work.

In light of these trends, the time is right for contemporary weavers to reaffirm our commitment to the simple structure of ancient textiles. Our modern advantages include more efficient looms, high-quality warp and weft yarns, and better communications, encouraging us to share problems, solutions, and everyday enthusiasms with other tapestry weavers. I believe that we can combine these recent developments with venerable techniques to create tapestries for the twenty-first century which will reflect a level of integrity equal to, or greater than, that of our ancestors.

Three tools for beating wefts: a large, weighted hand beater, a pointed bobbin, and an old, ivory lace bobbin. Photographed by George Goodwin.

An assortment of weft yarns, butterflies, and bobbins.

Weft yarns of primary and secondary hues (red, blue, yellow, green, orange, and violet) shown in low and high intensities.

A progression of values woven with warm and cool hues. In the black-and-white photograph, hues are lost but values remain.

About This Book

Students of weaving, perhaps because of their tactile inclinations, seem to prefer learning new methods through hands-on experience. As a rule, they would rather weave first and conceptualize later. Once they have acquired a frame of reference for which images can actually be woven and which cannot, they move on to create their own designs.

Thus, this book approaches tapestry by guiding you through the weaving of a handsome sampler about ten feet (three meters) long. Each section of the book provides step-by-step instructions for weaving one or more small examples of a single technique, allowing you to thoroughly explore its intricacies. As you experiment with one technique after another, your long sampler will take shape. When it is finished, it will be not only a much-admired achievement but a valuable reference—a woven record of the dozens of techniques that are now in your repertoire.

At the beginning of each section are "General Directions" for weaving the particular example; they recommend certain combinations of colors and explain how to execute the technique and its variations. The color assignments are not intended to be merely arbitrary or creatively limiting. On the contrary, they provide a sound visual context for further experimentation with color theories. In tapestry weaving, as in other two-dimensional art forms, contrasts between colors greatly influence the effects of a technique.

Following the "General Directions" are "Tips & Advice"—in-depth discussions of the broader aspects of the technique. Weaving a tapestry involves a series of decisions that can only be made by the weaver during the interpretive process. If you have a sound theoretical understanding of each technique, you can make those decisions in such a way that you maintain the integrity of the tapestry structure while you successfully interpret its design. Moreover, your original designs will be strongly influenced by your understanding of tapestry techniques, including their limitations and appropriate applications.

To take full advantage of the "Tips & Advice," read them completely before beginning to weave. Included may be useful step-by-step procedures for perfecting certain tapestry-weaving skills. These skills are acquired sequentially and in context. Some are relevant to only one specific technique, and others, such as entering or deleting a weft, are fundamental and used repeatedly throughout the weaving of the sampler. To avoid repetition, complete directions are given once for each weaving skill. Subsequent explanations assume that any previously explained skills are understood.

As you weave your way through this book, you will progress from fairly simple techniques, involving no more than three wefts, to the complexities of shading, outlining, and artistic expression. At the completion, you will have acquired what is needed to be a maker of tapestries: the necessary weaving skills; a working knowledge of our rich legacy of tapestry techniques; sound judgment about how to apply them; an understanding of color theory as it pertains to tapestry; and a direct, personal involvement with a deeply rewarding art form.

A Two-Harness Vertical Tapestry Loom

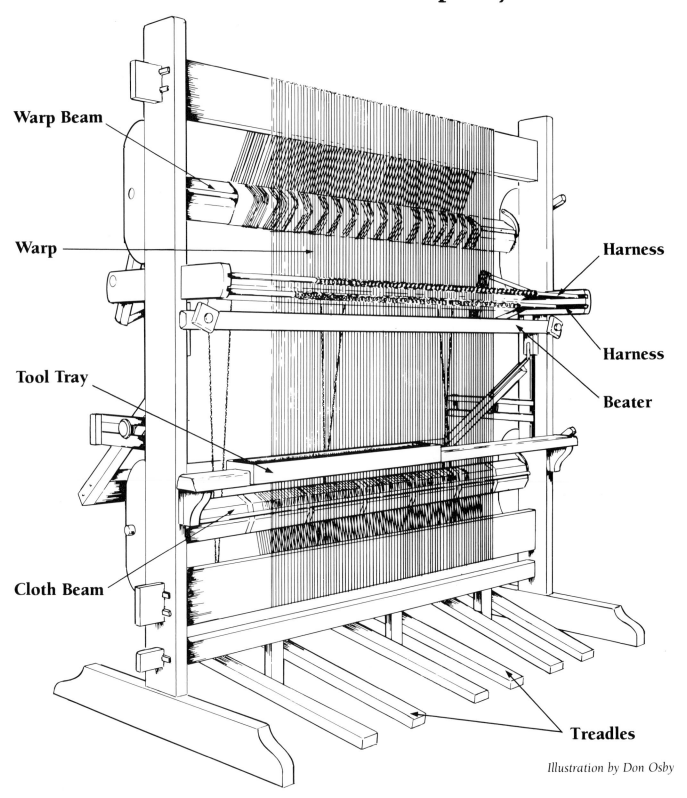

Warp Beam

Warp

Tool Tray

Cloth Beam

Harness

Harness

Beater

Treadles

Illustration by Don Osby

Beaming: Winding a warp onto the warp beam of a loom.

Beater: The swinging beam that holds the reed and packs the weft into the shed.

Fell: The position of the last row woven in a work in progress.

Reed: The removable part of the beater which spaces the warp and packs the weft.

Sett: The number of warp threads per inch.

Shed: An opening between two sets of warps through which weft yarns are passed.

13

Judy Chicago, The Creation of the World.
Woven by Audrey Cowan. 42" x 14' (105 cm.
by 4.25 m.); 1980 - 1984. Photo: Michele
Maier.

Constance Hunt, The Woven Woman. Cotton
warp; wool, pearl cotton weft; 10" x 10" (25 by
25 cm.); 1988. Photo: Gary Hunt. Collection
of Marianne Newton. San Mateo, California.

*Regine Bartsch, Seven Days. Linen warp,
wool weft; 55″ x 55″ (138 by 138 cm.); 1984.
Bartsch resides in County Kerry, Ireland.*

*Jan Yoors, Stampede. Woven by Annabert
and Marianne Yoors. Cotton warp, wool weft;
9′ x 12′ (2.7 by 3.7 m.); 1956. Photo: George
Cserna.*

Getting Started

Looms. Over the years, I have discovered that my students respond more positively to tapestry weaving if they can avoid struggling with wobbly frames, hazardous nails, troublesome warps, and inefficient shedding procedures. The process of creating a tapestry sampler is, in itself, challenging enough. Therefore, I recommend weaving the sampler described in this book on a floor loom, a sturdy table loom, or a vertical tapestry loom. The loom must accommodate the continuous five-yard (4.5-meter) warp required for sampling all the techniques and variations covered in the text. A shedding mechanism of some type accelerates the weaving process, allowing you to quickly observe the progression of each unique visual effect, while building a collection of examples at a satisfying, rather than a snail-like, pace. The reed controls the spacing of the warps as you dress the loom and advance the fell of the sampler. And the beater expedites the packing of rows woven across the full width of the warp.

The warp. A scrupulously installed tapestry warp of the highest quality yarn will function reliably and invisibly. First, choose a yarn that is smooth and evenly spun, has a high degree of tensile strength, and is invulnerable to the abrasive action of the reed. After much experimentation with various qualities of cotton and linen warp yarn, I can recommend 12/6 Fiskgarn-Mattvarp from Borgs, a tightly spun cotton twine. If that is unavailable, you can substitute cotton carpet warp, although it is not as strong.

Only skeletal warping instructions will be given here, focusing specifically on warp requirements for tapestry weaving. The diversity of looms recommended for weaving the sampler would necessitate printing complete instructions for several different warping procedures. If you should need further assistance, refer to one of the many excellent books containing comprehensive directions for dressing various types of looms. These references are listed in the bibliography.

On a standard warping board or reel, wind a warp (either the 12/6 Fiskgarn-Mattvarp or the carpet warp) at least five yards long. The tapestry sampler should measure 10″ (25 cm.) wide in the reed, sett at six ends per inch, but it should be woven on an uneven number of warps. Therefore, wind 61 ends, each of which measures at least five yards.

Dressing the loom. Dress the loom from either the front or the back, according to your preference. However, the beaming must be done with extreme care to ensure a perfectly even tension. Even slight variations in tension will result in exposed warps or puckers on the woven surface.

Since tapestry is woven tabby, or plain weave, thread the harnesses alternately if the loom has only two. If it has four harnesses, thread 1, 2, 3, 4, repeat. Tie up the harnesses to create the two alternate sheds: harness 1 against harness 2 on a two-harness loom, or harnesses 1 and 3 against harnesses 2 and 4 on a four-harness loom. The threading and tie-up should allow for the raising of even-numbered warps in one shed and odd-numbered warps in the alternate shed.

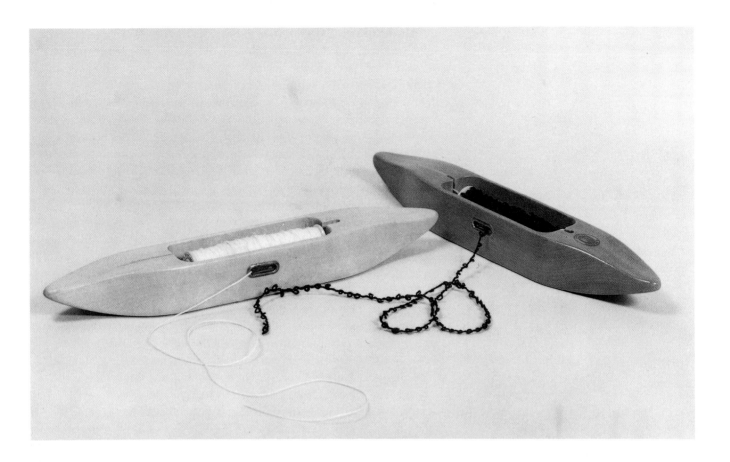

Preparing the warp. A tapestry warp requires certain initial preparations. As with any craft, laying a stable foundation prevents frustration later. The warp preparations serve to space the warps evenly, establish a reasonable width for the tapestry, construct a firm horizontal edge against which the first rows of tapestry can be beaten, and prepare the textile for its eventual finishing and mounting.

After dressing the loom, weave several rows alternating between the two tabby sheds, using heavy scrap yarn or rag strips as weft. Continue weaving until the warps are evenly spaced.

Next, weave about eight tabby rows using a fine, fuzzy yarn as weft. For this purpose, I keep the bobbin of a boat shuttle filled with inexpensive acrylic loop yarn. Any color can be used, because the yarn is eventually discarded. These rows of fuzzy yarn serve two purposes. First, as you weave them, the width of the fell will be gradually, nearly imperceptibly drawn in about ½″ (1.25 cm.). The mere action of weaving several rows of fine yarn through a coarse, widely spaced warp causes the overall width of the weaving to shrink. Do not yank the weft at the selvedges or distort the warps. Simply weave until the working width measures ½″ less than the width of the warp in the reed.

Most handweaving tends to draw in slightly. It seems to be an inevitable consequence of interweaving two different fibers. The amount of draw-in varies according to warp/weft proportions, warp and weft materials, the tension of the warp, and the weaver's personal style of handling the weft yarns. A draw-in of approximately ½″ is considered reasonable and acceptable for a tapestry 10″ wide. A wider tapestry may be drawn in as much as 2″ or 3″ (5 - 7.5 cm.). To control this phenomenon, establish a resolute width with the weaving of the crucial first rows—a width that can be comfortably sustained throughout the entire body of the tapestry.

Two boat shuttles with weft yarns that can be used at the beginning and end of a tapestry: fuzzy acrylic yarn (black) for establishing the tapestry's width, and warp yarn (white) for the headings.

The standard weaver's method of securing a weft tail at the beginning of the heading. Also visible are the rag strips for spacing the warp and the rows of fuzzy yarn for establishing the sett.

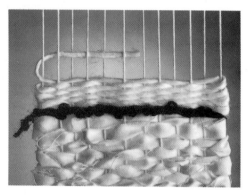

The standard weaver's method of securing a weft tail at the completion of the heading.

The heading. The second purpose of the rows of fuzzy yarn is to anchor the heading, a firmly woven foundation upon which the tapestry is constructed. A tapestry begins and ends with a heading. A small, lightweight tapestry requires simple headings about 1″ (2.5 cm.) wide, consisting of several tightly woven rows using warp yarn as weft. A very large, heavy tapestry warrants headings 2″ or 3″ wide, woven firmly using double or triple strands of warp yarn. The heading at the beginning of a tapestry provides a solid, straight edge upon which to build the initial rows. At the end, a heading provides a firm, horizontal conclusion over the final rows. Both headings serve to keep the knotted, trimmed warps folded to the back of the tapestry, and they guarantee straight, rolled edges at both ends. A mounting element can be anchored to a heading if the tapestry is mounted with its warps vertical. If the tapestry is mounted with its warps horizontal, the headings ensure that the sides of the tapestry hang straight. After the heading at the end of the sampler has been woven, it too should be secured with eight rows of fuzzy yarn.

To weave the heading of your tapestry sampler, wind either a boat shuttle or a stick shuttle with several yards of warp yarn. Weave the first pick (a single row of weaving) in either direction through either tabby shed, leaving a 4″ (10 cm.) tail protruding at the selvedge. Beat this row of weaving, but do not change the shed. To secure the weft tail, determine which is the last warp at this selvedge (the last warp may be either raised or lowered). Then carry the weft tail around this selvedge warp and back into the same shed as the first pick of weaving. Lay the tail over the weft in the shed for about 3″, and slip its cut end to the reverse side of the tapestry between two lowered warps. This is the conventional weavers' method for securing weft tails, useful in many instances for entering weft yarn at a selvedge.

Weave a heading 1″ wide, beating each row firmly before and after changing sheds. Develop the habit of placing the weft yarn through the shed at an upward angle before beating, to introduce a sufficient length for traveling over and under all warps. To construct neat selvedges, carefully stack each weft turn directly above the one below. Carry the weft yarn firmly around the selvedge warp. Loose wefts at this point result in unattractive loops at the selvedges. Observe the warps at the selvedges. They should never lose their parallel relationship, nor should they become drawn together. After the final pick of the heading has been woven, cut the weft yarn, leaving a 4″ tail protruding at the selvedge. Secure this weft tail in the same manner as before.

Note that, because you established the draw-in with the fuzzy yarn before weaving the heading, the heading will measure the same as the tapestry. A heading wider than the tapestry would protrude at the edges, since it is turned under during the finishing process.

Weft yarns. Next, gather a supply of weft yarns for weaving the sampler. The recommended wefts are fine, soft singles or two-ply wools, preferably yarns intended for weaving or needlework, rather than knitting or crochet. At least for the weaving of this sampler, avoid yarns with a great deal of surface fuzz and any that are unevenly spun. I prefer to use a three-strand Persian-type wool, as it can be used single (for a solid-color weft comprised of three strands), double (for a solid-color weft comprised of six strands), or individually in color-blended wefts, as the three strands may be easily separated. Three-strand Persian wool measures about 700 yards per pound, and one of the single strands about 2,000 yards per pound. Crewel yarn is another highly recommended tapestry wool, measuring 3,000 yards per pound. With any combination of these wools, a five- or six-strand weft should pack to completely cover the warp and sett assigned for this sampler.

Other wools of other weights may be used successfully, but the number of strands in the weft should be adjusted accordingly. Theoretically, the diameter of a tapestry weft, whatever number of strands may be included, should correspond to the size of the space between adjacent warps. Beaten against the previous row, a weft of this caliber should cover the warp completely. However, be prepared to adjust the weight of the weft to accommodate certain unpredictable variables, such as the sturdiness and weight of the loom, the maximum tension that can be applied to the warp, and the density of the weft yarn. If at any point during the weaving of the sampler you observe that the weft is not packing sufficiently to completely cover the warp, remove a single strand of yarn from your weft. In other words, gradually lighten the weight of the weft until you find the correct proportion.

Include in your palette of weft yarns a full range of values, especially the very lightest and the very darkest. "Value" refers to the relative lightness or darkness of a color. As it is used in this text, "hue" refers to the conventional name of a color (red, blue, pink, etc.). "Intensity" is the brightness or strength of a color. The hues of the weft yarns you select for your sampler are a matter of personal preference, but follow the specific recommendations for value and intensity. These contrasts have been assigned to demonstrate the use of color as a means of either emphasizing or moderating the visual effects of a technique.

Tapestry is usually woven using short lengths of weft yarn wound into the form of butterflies. A butterfly is made by stacking several figure eights of weft yarn between your thumb and smallest finger and securing them with a half-hitch knot. From this convenient hank, you can draw out any length you need, leaving the rest in a neat, untangled state. About four or five yards is the maximum amount to wind into a butterfly. Making large butterflies wastes time. They tend to tangle as the yarn is drawn out or become impossibly loose as the yardage diminishes.

Tapestry bobbins can also be used for controlling the wefts during the weaving process. Simply wind the strands of weft yarns around the bobbin and secure them with a knot. The knot prevents the bobbin from unrolling while allowing the yarn to be drawn out as needed. Many tapestry weavers prefer bobbins to butterflies. They are quick and easy to wind, and the point of a bobbin is conveniently at hand for packing the weft. The choice between butterflies and bobbins is a matter of personal preference, and either may be used for weaving this sampler. But since most tapestry weaving students own a minimum of expensive equipment, individual weft sources will be referred to as butterflies.

Another choice every tapestry weaver must eventually make is whether to weave from the front or the back of a tapestry. Traditionally, most tapestries have been woven from the back, to protect the front surface from soil and abrasion during the lengthy weaving process, and because certain valuable techniques can be executed only with the back of the tapestry facing the weaver. On the other hand, many contemporary weavers prefer to work from the front of their tapestries, where they can see their images take shape and adapt their techniques accordingly. Eventually, you should consider your type of loom as well as your preferred weaving technique. For now, weave the sampler from the front. The weaving will proceed more efficiently, and the examples will be visible immediately.

Making a butterfly.

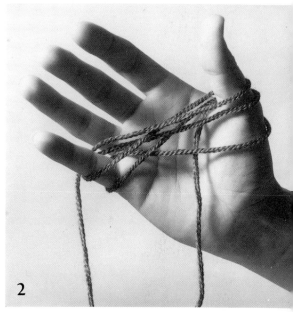

1

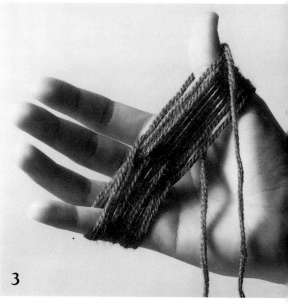

2

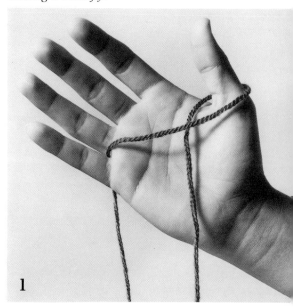

3

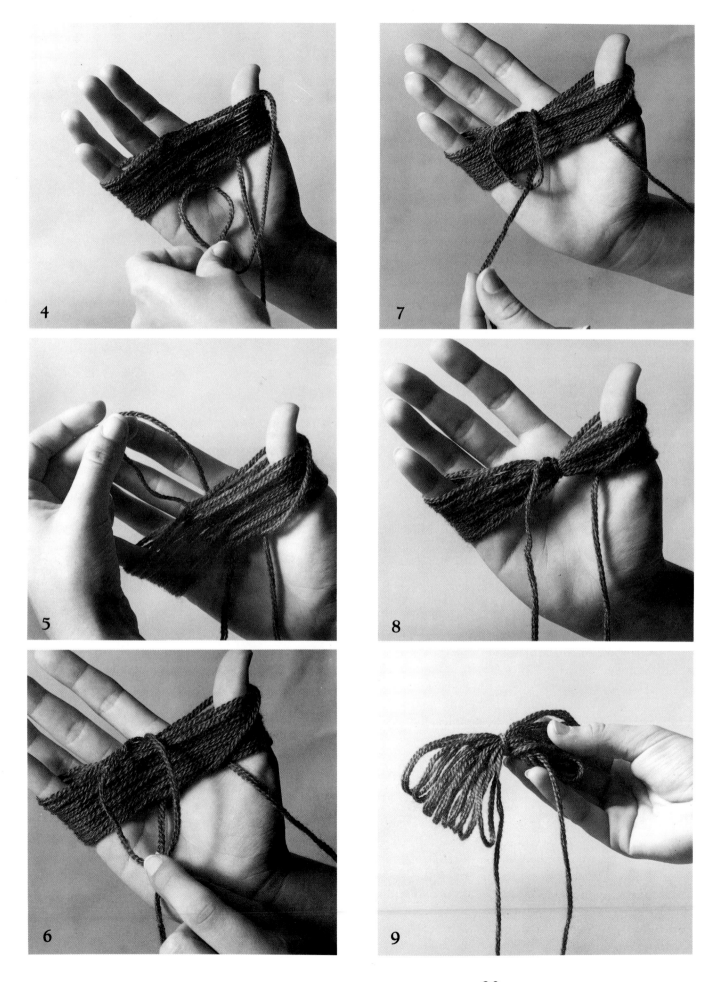

Basic Tapestry Technique

1

By this time you have probably leafed through the entire book, scanning the rich and varied array of tapestries illustrating the text. It can be mind-boggling for a beginning tapestry student to examine these exciting works of art and try to imagine how they were woven. Tapestry differs from other media in that images are not merely applied to a surface; they are the surface, the structure, and the selvedges. Splashes of color, expressive and irregular in shape, leap from a contrasting background; yet, at close range you can see the skillfully woven integration of both color areas. Tiny flecks of color appear to be sprinkled randomly over an evenly woven sky; but, close up, you observe that the yarns of both the flecks and the sky contribute to the woven structure.

I can imagine your numerous questions. They have been asked of me by other students over the years. What is it about tapestries that enables them to survive for centuries? How is it possible to accurately and simultaneously place several colors of yarn into a woven structure? Are there certain design elements that cannot be described effectively in tapestry? Which aspects of the craft are loom-controlled and which are controlled by the weaver? Is it possible to interpret designs spontaneously or must everything be predetermined? As you weave your way through the sampler in this book, the techniques of tapestry weaving will become less mysterious, and you will have the answers to these and many other questions.

While the structure of tapestry weave is quite simple, developing specific contours with discontinuous wefts in a manner that does not compromise the structure cannot possibly be easy. But as you begin to understand the tapestry techniques, their requisite weaving skills, and their relationship to the structure of the textile, you will discover that the process of learning tapestry weaving need never be intimidating or frustrating.

Chapter One introduces basic tapestry technique by explaining how to create a weft-face textile of the highest quality. In the process, you also begin to build a useful collection of technical skills and to develop an informed, analytical visual sense.

Using a Single Weft

General Directions

Choose a weft yarn of any hue or intensity. Its value should be from the middle range, neither very dark nor very light. Make a butterfly with this weft yarn.

Into the next shed, enter the butterfly at either selvedge and secure its tail. As you recall, tabby (or plain weave) is almost always used for tapestry: Odd-numbered warps are raised to create one shed, and even-numbered warps are raised to create the opposite shed. Weave a section of basic tapestry weave, alternating between the two plain weave sheds. Beat firmly before and after changing sheds. Your example should measure about 2″ (5 cm.) from the end of the heading to the end of the first section. Complete the weaving of the example at either selvedge, and again secure the tail of the butterfly.

The author's method of securing a weft tail at a selvedge at the beginning of a woven area.

The author's method of securing a weft tail at a selvedge at the end of a woven area.

Tips & Advice

Securing weft tails. As you weave the first and last rows of this example, secure the tails of the weft yarn. The standard weaver's method for doing so is described in the introductory instructions for preparing the heading. While it is technically acceptable to enter or delete tapestry weft using this method, a short length of double weft is unavoidably introduced into a shed at the selvedge. Exposed warps can sometimes be an unattractive and frustrating consequence of areas of double weft. If the tension of the warp is very tight and the weft yarn very soft, weaving and beating several subsequent rows may eventually cover these exposed warps. If not, there is an alternative procedure for entering or deleting a butterfly at a selvedge which invisibly secures its tail, steers the tail away from the edge of the tapestry, and avoids placing double weft into a shed.

This procedure also involves carrying the weft tail around the selvedge warp and back into the same shed over the previous weft, but only over one or two lowered warps—at which point the tail should be dropped to the reverse side of the tapestry, and looped across the back for about 3″ (7.5 cm.). At this point, the tail may be locked again over a single lowered warp, leaving a 3″ length of weft dangling from the reverse side of the tapestry.

By securing butterfly tails in this manner, the usual 2″ to 3″ span of double weft yarn at the selvedge has been cleverly bypassed; the edge of the tapestry has been firmly woven, and with a consistent texture; and the tail has been securely and invisibly locked over a single remote warp. The weft yarn looped across the back of the tapestry poses no visual or structural problems, and the tail dangling from the single, securing warp should be tied to another tail during the finishing process. The carefully calculated weft-face proportions of tapestry seldom permit wide or excessive areas of double weft in any given shed, but it is possible to finesse minute amounts of strategically placed double weft.

Bubbling. As each row of weft is beaten against the previous row, the yarn makes a rather intricate journey, traveling over every other warp, and under each alternate warp. To ensure that the correct amount of weft yarn is introduced for these necessary actions, bubble the weft as it is carried through each shed. In other words, before the weft is beaten, it should resemble a series of semicircles created by laying the yarn loosely across the row and intermittently pushing it down with your fingers. Bubbling packs into a shed a length of weft substantially longer than the width of the tapestry.

Bubble the weft approximately every 2″ or 3″. You will quickly develop a reliable instinct for the amount of weft to be packed into each row. The best guideline is the appearance of the row after beating.

Bubbling too frequently or making bubbles too high packs an excess of weft yarn, causing irregular and unsightly bumps on the surface of the tapestry. Some bumps may disappear during the blocking process. Others, particularly those appearing as a loop of weft yarn, become a permanent part of the design. Excessive bubbling may also cause the warps to spread farther apart than their established sett, thus increasing the width of the tapestry.

On the other hand, bubbles that are too skimpy cause the tapestry to draw in across its width. This is an indication that the length of weft yarn beaten into the shed is insufficient. The slightly elastic weft chooses the path of least resistance, drawing the warps closer together. Watch carefully as the tapestry grows, checking that there is no distortion or narrowing of the spaces between the warps. Measure the width of the tapestry at frequent intervals.

Good bubbling technique. Bubbles have the right height and the right frequency across the row.

An effective bubbling technique is to draw down the weft yarn with two fingers around one or two raised warps, stopping slightly short of the fell. The two-finger technique distributes the lowest point of the weft over a slightly wider area. Therefore, you avoid overstuffing these low areas, or creating weft bumps.

Ideally, the weft yarn in each shed should be long enough to comfortably travel over and under every warp and to cover the warps completely, but not long enough to produce a lumpy or loopy surface. If, as your tapestry grows, you observe its width becoming narrower or its texture uneven, it may be worthwhile to unweave a few rows and adjust your bubbling technique. This can be time well spent—learning to refine the quality of basic tapestry weave.

Constructing a selvedge. At the beginning of each row of weaving, carry the weft yarn firmly around the warp at the selvedge. The edges of a tapestry should never be soft or loopy. Each weft turn should be positioned directly over the previous one. The weft must not become twisted at the selvedge; arrange the individual strands to lie neatly above one another. The warps at the selvedge should remain absolutely parallel. After the selvedge has been established, pack down the weft at this point with your fingers, stabilizing the weave at the edge of the tapestry. Begin bubbling the row without involving the packed weft near the selvedge. Using these guidelines, develop a consistent procedure for handling tapestry selvedges.

Replacing a butterfly. To replace a depleted butterfly, simply drop its tail (which should be at least 3″ long) to the back of the tapestry, between two lowered warps anywhere in the middle of the row. Then drop the tail of a new butterfly over the last lowered warp that the old butterfly covered, sending it through the shed in the correct direction.

Observe that both the departing and the newly arriving butterflies cover the same lowered warp, their tails dangling from opposite sides. During the finishing process, these two tails should be tied to one another on the back of the tapestry. The tiny amount of double weft over the single warp is quite invisible.

In a solid-color example such as this one, additional yarn may be added invisibly at any point along the row of weaving without affecting either the structure of the tapestry or its design. However, if possible, avoid making splices too close to a selvedge. A dangling weft tail too near the edge may eventually work its way into a position where it is visible from the front of the tapestry.

Using Multiple Wefts

General Directions

Choose a weft yarn of any hue or intensity with a very light value. The light value of the yarn emphasizes the slight change of texture caused by weft turns. The tiny shadows would be obscured in the weave of an example woven with a very dark yarn. Make three butterflies with this weft yarn.

Into the next shed, enter one of the butterflies at either selvedge. After securing its tail, weave this butterfly through the shed for a distance of about 3″. Then lift the butterfly out of the shed through the raised warps, and rest it on the woven surface. Bubble the weft as usual, but wait until the other two butterflies have been entered and woven before beating this row.

Enter the other two butterflies into the approximate center of the remaining width, by carrying their tails into the shed from opposite

A neatly woven selvedge. Each successive weft turn is placed directly above the one below.

Entering a new weft invisibly into the middle of a row of weaving.

Entering three wefts into a row, traveling in opposition to one another.

The second row of weaving. All three butterflies have reversed direction but are still in opposition.

The first pass: two adjacent wefts of the same color meeting between two adjacent raised warps.

directions and overlapping them over a single lowered warp. The tails should measure about 3″ long as they dangle from the back of the tapestry. These two butterflies travel away from each other, one to the nearest selvedge and the other to the same position as the first butterfly. In this position, there will be two butterflies emerging from between a pair of adjacent raised warps. Bubble the remaining two butterflies and beat the entire row.

Observe that each of the three butterflies has been woven through the shed in the direction opposite its adjacent butterfly. As each row is woven, the directions of all three butterflies will be reversed, but they should always be traveling in opposition to their neighbors.

Change sheds and weave the next row, reversing the directions of all three butterflies. The first to be woven in this row should be the butterfly from the emerging pair traveling toward a selvedge. This converging pair of butterflies will now relay. To "relay" means to reverse directions while touching gently in a space between adjacent warps. Note that between the pair of emerging butterflies is a raised warp. To correctly weave the first butterfly, carry it around this raised warp and through the shed to the selvedge. Bubble the weft of the first butterfly. This common raised warp must always be covered by one or the other of the pair of relaying butterflies. In a solid-color area, either butterfly may be carried around the raised warp. However, as the two butterflies enter the shed traveling away from each other, the tendency may be to ignore this warp, leaving it exposed. This is a weaving error resulting in the appearance of a small vertical white line (warp) on the surface of the tapestry.

Next, weave the middle butterfly across the row for about 2″ toward the third butterfly. The point at which this butterfly emerges from the shed determines the position of the next relay. Choose any position except that of the previous relay. Lift the middle butterfly out of the shed between the raised warps, bubble it, and rest it on the weaving surface.

The third butterfly should now be woven from the selvedge to meet the second butterfly between the same raised warps. Bubble the third butterfly and beat row two.

Continue weaving in this manner until the example measures about 3″. Each butterfly should be woven toward another butterfly, meeting it between adjacent raised warps, or it should be woven away from its neighbor toward a selvedge. End one of the butterflies as it is woven toward a selvedge. Secure its tail at the selvedge in the usual manner. The remaining two butterflies will meet at some point in the middle of the row. Overlap their tails over a single, lowered warp.

Tips & Advice

Choosing relays. From this point on, nearly all your tapestry weaving will be executed with more than one weft at a time. As wefts are relayed back and forth through the sheds, you will be faced with decisions directly affecting the quality and design of the tapestry. For instance, you must decide which weft of an emerging pair should be carried around the common raised warp. In a solid-color area, such as the example you have just woven, either butterfly may correctly cover this warp. But if contrasting weft colors are converging in a design, the correct color must be carried around the raised warp.

Another recurring decision is the choice of relay position for converging wefts. Again, as areas of contrasting color are introduced, your decisions will be guided by the design. But, in this example, focus your attention primarily on avoiding the vertical slits that result from relaying around the same two warps for several passes in succession. As you weave adjacent wefts toward each other, check the previous relay and establish the next in a different position. If you continually shift the positions of the relays, slits cannot develop.

Controlling texture. In the first example on your sampler, a single weft travels continuously from selvedge to selvedge, producing a regular and uninterrupted texture. But in the second example, woven with three discontinuous wefts, something different occurs. When a weft reverses direction in the middle of a row, the yarn is carried around a warp at a slight angle. This angled weft, however minute, appears in the weave as a slightly different texture. And by reversing adjacent wefts around adjacent warps, you create a tiny slit at the point of the relay, adding to the textural variation.

Although these inevitable textures cause only minor visual consequences, you should learn to control and modify their effects. For instance, as you reverse the direction of a weft, whether around a raised or a lowered warp, use only a moderate amount of tension. Pulling too tightly at this point will distort the warp, leaving a small gap in the weave. On the other hand, executing weft turns in an extremely loose or sloppy manner creates unsightly bumps on the surface of the tapestry.

Even if your weft turns have the perfect degree of tension, there is still a slightly different texture to solid-color areas woven with multiple wefts. Why, then, do we not simply weave with a single weft all the way across a solid-color area? One reason is that wefts can be passed through the shed from hand to hand more easily if they are required to travel across only narrow areas. But the most important reason is consistency of technique and quality control of the weave. For instance, if one or more areas of a tapestry design require the manipulation of several wefts, all of a different color, a certain quality of weave is established in these areas. The essence of this quality and its effect on the width and selvedges of the tapestry are determined by the relaying actions of the group of wefts. Therefore, to keep the quality of the weave consistent throughout a tapestry and to effectively control its width and selvedges, all solid-color areas above, below, or beside a patterned area must be woven with a similar number of wefts, relaying in a similar manner.

Break wide, solid-color areas into several smaller, relaying areas, particularly important when setting up the first row, as it is here that the quality of the weave and the width of the tapestry are established. About 10″ (25 cm.) is the maximum width to weave successfully with a single weft. If the first rows of your tapestry describe a solid-color background area 60″ (150 cm.) wide, set up the first row of weaving with at least six butterflies, all the same color and traveling in opposition to one another.

Lazy lines and random relays. It is possible to create a subtle pattern throughout a solid-color background by carefully placing weft relays. The Navajo weavers (and many other contemporary weavers) refer to these configurations as "lazy lines." Lazy lines are diagonal arrangements of weft relays, created by regularly shifting the position of each relay in a series either one warp to the left or one warp to the right. Reversing the direction of the lazy line at regular intervals results in a distinctive diamond pattern.

As wefts converge, lift them out of the shed at the point you have chosen for the next relay. Note that the position of a relay is determined as two wefts are woven toward each other, and the relay itself is executed as the wefts travel away from each other. By directing the actions of the wefts in this manner, you can organize a series of relays in a regular pattern, creating a lazy line, or you can distribute them at random, as in your example. Either method will prevent slits in the weave.

The second pass: the right weft being reversed around the common raised warp.

Three techniques executed with five different values of weft yarns. Plain tapestry weave woven with a single weft (bottom), with two wefts relaying randomly (middle), and with two wefts relaying in a lazy line pattern (top).

Navajo Blanket, Chief Design. Cotton warp, single-spun wool weft; 55″ x 60″ (138 by 150 cm.). Photo: George Mauro. Collection of Carol and Ken Hopper. Stepped diagonals, Rolakan-type interlocks, lazy lines.

Claude, Arizona. Cotton warp, two-ply wool weft; 68″ x 76½″ (170 by 191 cm.); ca. 1957. Woven at Pinton Freres Tapisserie D'Aubusson. Photo: George Mauro. Collection of Diana Gast. Lazy lines, sewn slits.

BASIC TAPESTRY TECHNIQUE

Sylvia Ptak, 1941—Baggage, Destination Unknown, #1. Linen warp; wool weft with metallic threads, chenille, and mohair; 42" x 32" (105 by 80 cm.); 1987. Photo: Jack Ramsdale.

Rose/Blue Stove Cover (Sofreh). Heavy, multiply cotton warp; handspun, single wool weft; 34" x 38" (85 by 95 cm.). Photo: George Mauro. Collection of Jason Nazmiyal/Rug & Kilim. Reversible tapestry weave with spontaneous relays between contrasting wefts; heavily weighted on all four sides, probably for stability and heat retention.

Elaine Ireland, Red Tulips. Woven by the artist and Pamela Hardesty-O'Sullivan. Cotton warp, wool weft; 44″ x 48″ (110 by 120 cm.); 1984.

Susan Hart Henegar, Zzz . . . Cotton warp, wool weft; 72″ x 48″ (180 by 120 cm.); 1985. Four-color pinstripe in center background, post-modern theme.

Pick-and-Pick Techniques

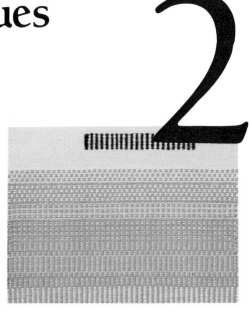

T he narrow vertical stripes of pick-and-pick are universally recognizable: weft-face stripes created by the complementary actions of those invisible but crucial warps. Weaving one weft color through one of the two sheds, and a contrasting weft color through the opposite shed, causes a horizontal alternation of the two weft colors. Pick-and-pick stripes are developed by stacking row upon row of alternating dots of weft colors.

Interpreted in highly contrasting colors, pick-and-pick boldly describes stripes or geometric patterns; woven in closely related colors, pick-and-pick results in elusive, shimmering textures.

This technique has been placed near the beginning of the tapestry sampler to help train your eyes and hands to recognize and use the two weaving sheds efficiently. By weaving with two contrasting colors, you can easily determine the correct shed and the correct weft color for each row. Since mistakes are emphasized by the color contrast, they can be corrected immediately.

In addition, you will begin to learn about the specific color effects of each tapestry technique—a most important aspect of the sampler described in this book. Weft-face textiles require a specialized approach to color theory. The specific interlacings and resulting visual effects of each tapestry technique are greatly influenced by your choice of weft colors and the degree of contrast between them. Each woven example provides valuable practice with a different set of inseparable technical and color interactions.

Contrasting values.   *Similar values.*

Basic Pick-and-Pick

General Directions

Choose two weft yarns of any hue. One yarn should be of a dark value, the other very light or very bright. The two colors should contrast sharply. Make a butterfly with each of these weft yarns.

Into the next shed, enter the darker butterfly at either selvedge. Weave it to the opposite selvedge, then bubble and beat the row. Change sheds, enter the lighter butterfly traveling in the same direction, weave it to the opposite selvedge, and bubble and beat again.

Continue weaving with the two butterflies following each other in opposite sheds. The example of this technique should measure about 2″ (5 cm.) wide. To keep the stripes uncluttered, end each of the butterflies in its last row.

Observe the well-defined vertical stripes. Weaving a color through the same shed, every other row, builds vertical stripes of the color over the warps lowered in that shed. Weaving a contrasting color through the opposite shed, every alternate row, builds vertical stripes of that color over the alternate warps.

If you could turn the weaving over, you would see that the colors of the stripes on the back are the reverse of those on the front. Look closely at the weaving structure. As the weft is beaten, it covers alternate warps on one side of the tapestry and the opposite alternate warps on the reverse side of the tapestry. A weft-face textile requires two rows of weft to completely cover every warp—which is why tapestry weavers refer to two rows (or picks) of weaving as one complete pass.

The beginning of pick-and-pick selvedge technique: two butterflies at the same selvedge.

The first procedure for weaving selvedge stripes. The selvedge warp is raised.

The second procedure for weaving selvedge stripes. The selvedge warp is lowered.

Tips & Advice

Weaving selvedge stripes. Selvedges require special consideration when weaving with two butterflies in opposite sheds. The warps at either selvedge, like all other warps along the row, should be covered by only one of the weft colors, thus retaining the clarity and rhythm of the stripes. If you cross the two wefts at the selvedges, carrying both butterflies around the selvedge warps, the colors will mingle, creating unnecessary visual clutter. Two weaver's tricks—one for a raised selvedge warp, the other for a lowered one—can keep your selvedges clean.

1. If both butterflies are at one selvedge, the shed has been opened for weaving the next row, and the selvedge warp is *raised,* then the yarn of the next butterfly to be woven should be underneath the selvedge warp, and the yarn of the other butterfly should be over the selvedge warp.

Carry the active butterfly over the yarn of the resting butterfly, under the selvedge warp, and into the shed. Tug slightly on the yarn of the active butterfly, causing the yarn of the resting one to slip around the selvedge warp. This maneuver also steers the yarn of the active butterfly over the second warp from the selvedge, its correct position for the row. Note that the active butterfly has completely avoided the selvedge warp. Bubble and beat this row.

Change sheds, and weave the second butterfly. As this butterfly is carried into the shed, it automatically makes a second trip over the selvedge warp, compensating for this warp's being skipped by the first butterfly. Bubble and beat this row. Observe the neat progression of vertical stripes. Each warp, including the selvedge warp, is neatly covered by only one weft color. (The reverse side of the tapestry will have a double-width stripe of one color along the selvedge, but the right side of the tapestry will be perfect.)

2. If both butterflies are at one selvedge, the shed has been opened for weaving the next row, and the selvedge warp is *lowered,* then the yarn of the next butterfly to be woven should be over the selvedge warp, and the yarn of the other butterfly should be under the selvedge warp. In these circumstances, the next butterfly to be woven should be the one covering the selvedge warp. First, in order to avoid crossing the two yarns, place the resting butterfly out of the way on the woven surface—not on the unwoven warps. Wrap the active butterfly twice around the lowered selvedge warp. After the second wrap, carry it through the shed, all the way across the row. Two wraps of the selvedge warp with the first color compensate for its being skipped by the second color. Bubble and beat this row, and change sheds for the next.

The second butterfly can be woven through the shed with no special manipulation. Notice that it completely avoids the selvedge warp. Bubble and beat this row.

Again, this procedure creates perfect selvedge stripes only if the tapestry is being woven from the right side. When weaving pick-and-pick designs on a reversible textile, the two weft yarns should be neatly crossed at the selvedges.

As you weave the pick-and-pick variations in the next sections, you will learn to switch the positions of the stripes, changing the circumstances at the selvedges. This will give you valuable experience with both procedures for weaving selvedge stripes.

Uneven number of warps. If you dress the loom with an uneven number of warps, both selvedge warps will be either raised or lowered, requiring the same procedure for creating neat selvedge stripes. Another advantage to planning pick-and-pick areas on an uneven number of warps is that both selvedges are covered by the same color, balancing the design.

Entering and deleting wefts. Take care as you enter a new color or replace a depleted butterfly. Weft tails must be handled so that they don't intrude over or around any warps that are the sole territory of the other color. Look carefully at the previous row and avoid introducing a color over any warps, including a selvedge warp, belonging to the stripe sequence of the other color. The same caution would apply to ending a color of yarn. In this case, carefully end a weft after its last row, not after the entire pick-and-pick area is complete.

Choosing a procedure. You may develop a preference for one or the other of the two ways of handling selvedge stripes. For instance, when weaving pick-and-pick from selvedge to selvedge, I prefer the second procedure because it results in neat, flat selvedges with no tendency to curl. However, when inserting a small area of pick-and-pick into a tapestry, I prefer the first procedure because it is easier to work around a raised warp in the middle of a row. If you have similar preferences, begin your area of pick-and-pick in whichever shed is the correct one for the procedure you prefer.

Offset Pick-and-Pick

General Directions

A donkey bag showing offset pick-and-pick. Photographed by George Goodwin.

Choose two colors of weft yarn with contrasting hues and values. One or both of the colors should be different from those used for the first pick-and-pick example. Make a butterfly with each of these weft yarns.

As you proceed with the weaving of the tapestry sampler, you will be choosing many contrasting pairs of colors. Try to combine as many different colors as possible. The visual references provided by various interactions between hues, values, and intensities should prove extremely valuable in planning and evaluating color relationships for future projects.

In the same manner as the previous example, weave about ½″ of pick-and-pick stripes. Then weave two consecutive rows with one color. This interrupts the vertical stripes with a horizontal line, while switching the positions of the colors. The darker yarn will now cover the warps previously covered by the lighter yarn and vice versa. Continue weaving, making at least three or four shifts. The example for this section should measure about 3″ (7.5 cm.). As you weave, consider the numerous applications of this technique.

Tips & Advice

Switching stripes. As you switch the positions of the two weft colors, you also switch the color of the stripes at the selvedges. Begin immediately to build neat selvedge stripes after each shift of position, using one of the procedures described earlier.

To switch the positions of the stripes, you must weave two consecutive rows with one butterfly while the other butterfly rests for two rows. Observe the last row woven with the resting butterfly. If its yarn is under the selvedge

warp, the weft may be carried vertically on the reverse side of the tapestry to begin the next pick-and-pick row. But if its yarn is over the selvedge warp, carrying the weft vertically to the next pick-and-pick row would create an unacceptable loop on the surface of the tapestry. In this case, to neatly position both colors for resuming pick-and-pick above a horizontal line, carry the yarn of the resting butterfly vertically along the selvedge warp, and surround it with the yarn of the butterfly being used to weave the two-row horizontal stripe. Both weft yarns will emerge above the horizontal line with no mingling of the two colors at the selvedge.

You have now been introduced to a clever technique for invisibly carrying a weft yarn along a selvedge. This time, the yarn was hidden under only one row of weaving, but it is also possible to carry a weft yarn for several rows, while retaining a neat, solid-color selvedge. The technique is especially useful if a pick-and-pick area is frequently interrupted by horizontal lines, as will be the case in the next two sections. If one of the colors of weft yarn needs to wait for a few rows, simply carry it along the selvedge, and weave the other color around it for as many rows as required. The hidden yarn may emerge at any point to reenter the weave.

Applications. Consider the visual effect of the two consecutive rows separating the sections of pick-and-pick. Weft colors and their values must be very carefully chosen for weaving emphatic design elements such as horizontal lines.

Give some thought to the various patterns you could create with offset pick-and-pick. By carefully controlling the lengths of the vertical stripes, you could weave mathematically regular patterns. Or by switching the positions of the stripes at random, you could create an interrupted, free-form design.

Pick-and-Pick as a Grid Pattern

General Directions

Again, select two colors of weft yarn with a very high degree of contrast, and make a butterfly with each.

With the darker butterfly, weave either three or four rows, ending in whichever shed places dark weft over both selvedge warps. In other words, the last row woven with the darker butterfly, whether it is its third or fourth row, should be in the shed with both selvedge warps lowered. This ensures that the darker color will form borders at the top, bottom, and sides of this example, as well as the horizontal and vertical interstices of the grid.

Change sheds, enter the lighter butterfly at either selvedge, and weave pick-and-pick until the lighter stripe is as high as it is wide. This should take two to four rows, depending upon your beating style and the weight of the weft yarn. Then weave three more rows of the darker color over the row of squares. Build at least three more rows of grids in this manner. End the lighter weft after its last row, and finish the example with three rows of the darker color. End the darker weft.

Weave the section again, reversing the positions of the two values. This time, the four borders and both the horizontal and vertical interstices will be light, and the squares within the grid will be dark. Compare the effects of the two examples.

Seventh- or eighth-century Coptic tapestry, probably Egyptian, with pick-and-pick as part of the pattern. Collection of the Textile Museum, Washington, D.C.

Tips & Advice

Resuming pick-and-pick. Observe that, in every pick-and-pick sequence, the weft used for weaving the squares within the grid begins and ends over a lowered warp just inside the selvedge. In fact, this weft travels exclusively inside the selvedges. Therefore, to neatly resume a pick-and-pick sequence after a horizontal stripe, carry this weft vertically on the reverse side of the tapestry over each horizontal stripe.

Consistency. Count the rows of pick-and-pick required to build the small squares. Use this count and an even beating style to keep the squares consistent.

Solid lines. It is important to understand why three rows must be woven to create the solid line between the pick-and-pick squares. Recall that one pick of a color covers every other warp, creating a dotted line or one half of a complete pass. Two picks of a color cover every warp, resulting in a solid line while switching the colors of pick-and-pick stripes. Therefore, three picks create the narrowest possible horizontal line without switching the positions of the vertical stripes.

Distinguishing sheds. A tapestry weaver must eventually be able to recognize at a glance which of the two sheds is the correct one for any number of weaving circumstances. The complicated but logical execution of these pick-and-pick examples provides valuable practice with distinguishing between the two sheds and managing their inseparable functions.

Tapestry weaving will always be a time-consuming craft, but with experience, weavers develop facility with certain familiar chores. To gain this facility, the most useful tools are your eyes and your hands. Your eyes are being trained to see all of the circumstances on the loom, enabling you to make quick, accurate judgments, and your hands are being trained to do all manipulations skillfully and economically.

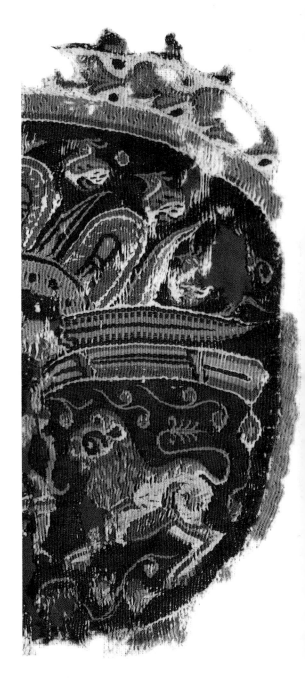

Pick-and-Pick as a Honeycomb Pattern

General Directions

Select another pair of contrasting colors of weft yarn, and make a butterfly with each. Weave two picks with the darker yarn. Enter the lighter yarn and weave pick-and-pick for as many rows as it takes to square the narrow stripes. Weave two more rows of darker weft, creating a solid horizontal line above the row of squares, while switching the positions of the pick-and-pick blocks. Again weave pick-and-pick until the stripes are square; then weave two more darker rows. Continue weaving in this manner for about 1½″ (3.75 cm.), building row upon row of offset squares. Notice the honeycomb effect.

Reverse the values and weave another small example. This time, the framework of the honeycomb will be woven with the lighter weft, and the little squares inside the framework will be woven with the darker weft.

The pick-and-pick possibilities woven on a sett of 6 e.p.i.

Entering two wefts into the middle of a row by overlapping their tails over a common lowered warp.

Tips & Advice

Selvedges. Weave the pick-and-pick rows according to the instructions in the first part of this chapter. Otherwise, the selvedges require no special attention. With the honeycomb technique, blocks of both colors appear alternately along the selvedges.

Grid vs. honeycomb. This cleverly conceived, small-scale pattern lacks the rigid horizontal and vertical interstices of the grid described earlier. Consider the various applications of these two very different pick-and-pick patterns. Could the grid pattern be used to portray architectural elements, echo geometric shapes, or create bold stylizations? Could the honeycomb pattern be used to describe patterns in nature or perhaps the texture of a textile within a tapestry design? As you weave this and every other section of the tapestry sampler, be thinking of possible applications for each technique, and make notes of them for your future projects.

Inserting an Area of Pick-and-Pick Into the Background of a Tapestry

General Directions

Choose a color of weft yarn for the background of this example with a value from the middle range, neither very light nor extremely dark. Make two butterflies. Next, choose two colors of weft yarn for the pick-and-pick area, and make a butterfly with each of these. One weft color should be selected from your very lightest values and the other from your very darkest ones. The two pick-and-pick colors should contrast with each other, as well as with the background. The hues and/or intensities of the three yarns may also contrast, emphasizing the extremes of value. But the most important contrasts should be between the lightest, middle, and darkest values.

Open the shed for weaving the next row, and enter the two background butterflies traveling in opposite directions toward the selvedges. Overlap the wefts from opposite directions over one or two lowered warps in the approximate middle of the row, leaving 3″ tails dangling from the reverse side of the tapestry. Bubble the two butterflies and beat the row.

This is the usual method for entering two wefts of the same color into the middle of a row. It is similar to the procedure for adding a new yarn source in the middle of a row. The small overlap of weft yarn in the shed will not cause exposed warps, and the two tails on the back of the tapestry will be tied to each other during the finishing process. Two wefts of the same color may also be deleted from a tapestry in much the same manner—simply overlap their tails from opposite directions over one or two lowered warps.

With the two background butterflies, weave about 1″ (2.5 cm.) of basic tapestry weave. As in Chapter One, they should meet between adjacent raised warps in every other shed and return to the selvedges in the alternate sheds. Remember to distribute the relays, to avoid creating slits. End this inch of background with the two butterflies resting at the selvedges. Do not cut the yarns at this time.

Open the shed for the next row of weaving. Designate a 3″-wide block of warps on which to weave the pick-and-pick area. Remember that, to balance the colors of the pick-and-pick selvedges, the area should be woven on an uneven number of warps. Therefore, raised warps should form both selvedges. Using a permanent marker, make small marks directly onto these two raised warps, close to the reed, for easy identification.

Enter the lightest butterfly, traveling in either direction, across only the pick-and-pick area. Carry it under both marked warps and out of the shed, and rest it on the surface of the tapestry. Secure the tail of this weft in the same manner as you would at a pick-and-pick selvedge, avoiding the marked warp, which should be covered only by the darkest color of yarn. Bubble the yarn of this butterfly, but do not beat.

Next, weave the two background butterflies from the selvedges toward the pick-and-pick section. One of the background butterflies will meet the lightest butterfly between two raised warps, and the other will weave to the pick-and-pick section, traveling in the same direction as the lightest butterfly. Bubble the background butterflies and beat the row.

Change sheds and enter the darkest butterfly across only the pick-and-pick section, traveling in the same direction as the lightest butterfly. Carry this butterfly out of the shed, rest it on the surface of the tapestry, and secure its tail around the marked warp. Bubble the yarn, but do not beat until both background butterflies have been woven in this row.

Next, weave the two background butterflies toward the tapestry selvedges. As they enter the shed from the edge of the pick-and-pick area, be sure to check two things: (1) that the background butterflies are covering (or traveling around) only background warps, not pick-and-pick warps; and (2) that the background butterflies have not skipped any background warps.

You will now be weaving with four selvedges: the two of the tapestry, and the two of the pick-and-pick area. Continue weaving in this manner, until the pick-and-pick area measures about 1″ vertically. Weave the darkest butterfly all the way across the pick-and-pick area in one shed, and the lightest butterfly all the way across the pick-and-pick area in the opposite shed. Weave the two background butterflies in every shed, alternately weaving toward the selvedges and toward the pick-and-pick area.

End the pick-and-pick area one color at a time. In other words, immediately after you have woven the last row with the lightest butterfly, end it. Then weave the final pick-and-pick row with the darkest butterfly and end it. With both pick-and-pick butterflies deleted and secured, the two background butterflies may now be woven toward each other, over the pick-and-pick area, relaying between any two raised warps. Weave ½″ (1.25 cm.) of background above the pick-and-pick area. End the two background butterflies in the approximate middle of the row, by over-lapping their tails from opposite directions over one or two lowered warps.

Next, choose two weft yarns with very closely related hues and values. To compare the values of two hues, stand near a north-facing window, holding several strands of both colors of yarn in your hand, and squint at them. Squinting is a quick and easy way of evaluating the degree of contrast between values. As in a black and white photograph, the squinting action of your eyes erases most of the hue, leaving only the relative lightness or darkness of the two colors. In this case, squinting should result in your observation of two very closely related grays. Make a butterfly with each of these weft yarns.

Again weave small examples of each of the pick-and-pick techniques, using closely related colors of weft yarn. Experiment with different pairs,

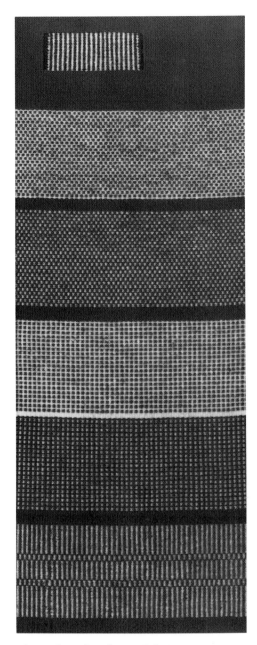

The pick-and-pick possibilities woven on a sett of 10 e.p.i.

Deleting two wefts in the middle of a row by overlapping their tails over a common lowered warp.

each exploring a unique interaction of colors. Observe how these value relationships, very different from those of the original pick-and-pick examples, have reduced the strong patterns to subtle, shimmering textures. How might you apply these exciting possibilities to your tapestry designs?

Tips & Advice

Selvedge stripes. With the shed open for weaving the first row of the pick-and-pick area, you selected two raised warps designating its selvedges. And by choosing raised warps, as opposed to lowered ones, you set up the correct circumstances for using the first of the two procedures for weaving selvedge stripes, described earlier in the chapter. While either procedure will work in an inserted pick-and-pick area, the first procedure is usually the better choice. Building neat, solid-color selvedge stripes in the middle of a tapestry is much easier when working around warps that are conveniently raised.

Testing the marker. Before using a marker on the warps, be sure to test the ink for permanency. After making a large mark on a scrap of warp yarn, wet it thoroughly with hot water, and place it between several layers of wet, white paper towels. Allow the towels and the yarn to dry thoroughly. If the ink on the warp has not bled and there is no evidence of ink on the paper towels, the marker is safe to use.

The lightest butterfly. Each time you weave the lightest butterfly, be sure to weave it all the way across the pick-and-pick section and under the marked warp before lifting it out of the shed. Even though this butterfly does not travel around the marked warp, it must be in this position to correctly execute the procedure for weaving the selvedge stripe.

Slits. Examine the slits at both sides of the pick-and-pick area. You will be learning much more about slits in Chapter Three. But, basically, slits occur when adjacent butterflies reverse directions around the same two adjacent warps for several rows. These slits were intentionally created for two reasons: (1) because a pick-and-pick area is most effective if it is set off sharply from the background; and (2) because most of the techniques for preventing slits along a vertical line are incompatible with the procedures for weaving solid-color pick-and-pick selvedge stripes.

Weaving pick-and-pick separately. It is possible to weave the pick-and-pick area independently of the background. After you have woven the bottom of the background, weave the entire pick-and-pick area at one time, while the two background butterflies rest at the selvedges. Then weave the background areas at the sides, one at a time, beating with a hand beater or a fork. The loom beater should be used only for beating complete rows.

After both sides of the background have been woven to the top of the pick-and-pick area, weave the two background butterflies to meet over the pick-and-pick section. At this point the loom beater may again be used. Finish the section as directed.

There are two advantages to weaving this section separately: You can clearly see the two warps at the selvedges of the pick-and-pick area, and you can concentrate completely on weaving a neat, precise pick-and-pick section. On the other hand, you do not see the row-by-row relationship between the pick-and-pick section and the background (possibly causing a crooked or an exaggerated slit), and you may weave the wrong number of rows in one or both of the background sections.

The artist needs to learn how to translate the ambient light and dark of the real and/or imagined world into the light and dark patterns, or values, of design. Because we respond to value relationships in a predictably primitive, often subliminal way, learning to use value gives the artist a powerful tool for communication. It is the most important element in color design.

—Patricia Lambert

Linda Hutchins, Rubicon. Linen warp; wool, goat hair, and linen weft; 37″ x 38″ (93 by 95 cm.); 1989. Photo: Bill Bachhuber. Pick-and-pick as a grid pattern.

Small tapestry with pick-and-pick. Photo: Carmelina Margaret D'Amelio. Collection of Mary D'Amelio.

PICK-AND-PICK TECHNIQUES

Soyoo Hyunjoo Park, Bridge. Wool warp and weft; 72″ x 48″ (180 by 120 cm.); 1988. Photo: George Mauro. Pick-and-pick.

PICK-AND-PICK TECHNIQUES   38

Julia Mitchell, Rocks in a Brook. Linen warp, wool and silk weft; 60" x 43" (150 by 108 cm.); 1981. Pick-and-pick stripes, eccentric wefts.

Constance Hunt, The Ribbon Woman. *Cotton warp; wool, silk, and pearl cotton weft; 78″ x 69″ (195 by 173 cm.); 1989. Photo: Gary Hunt.*

Weft Relays and Crossings

3

The techniques explored in Chapter Three illustrate the difference between tapestry weaving and other types of weaving. Unlike wefts that are shuttled from selvedge to selvedge, discontinuous tapestry wefts travel back and forth within the contours of the artist's images, either touching gently in the spaces between the warps or crossing securely in some manner. These interactions between adjacent tapestry wefts affect not only the structural integrity of the textile but the style of its design interpretation. Thus, it is imperative to master the relays and crossings uniquely characteristic of the art of tapestry weaving.

In this chapter, beginning weavers can explore, step by step, the various techniques for connecting adjacent colors of weft or for shifting them around. Experienced weavers will discover new variations, refinements, and applications. After weaving the examples, both will have a record of the visual idiosyncrasies of each technique.

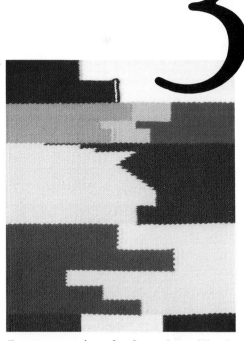

Entering two colors of weft into the middle of a row, for two well-defined areas of color.

Basic Slit Technique

General Directions

Choose three contrasting hues of weft yarn, and make a butterfly with each.

Enter all three butterflies into the next weaving shed, traveling in opposition to one another. One butterfly should be entered at either selvedge and woven toward the center. The other two should be entered at any point in the middle of the row—one traveling toward the first butterfly, the other toward the opposite selvedge. The exact positions of the three butterflies are not matters of great importance to the design of this example, but the relays of the three butterflies do determine where the two slits will be. One slit will develop between the center butterfly and the butterfly to its left; the other will fall between the center butterfly and the butterfly to its right.

Weave at least 16 rows with the three butterflies. The center butterfly and the one to its left should meet every other row, between the same pair of raised warps. In the alternate rows, they should reverse their directions, creating a slit between the two colors. The center butterfly and the butterfly at the right should meet in the alternate rows, creating a second slit as they reverse directions. All three butterflies should relay around the same warps every time they separate, stacking weft around those warps in the same manner as at the selvedges. Observe the three woven areas, each of a different solid color, separated by clean, straight vertical lines.

After you have woven about 1" (2.5 cm.) of this example, shift the two slits and the edges of the three color areas by moving the relays of the butterflies. Position the new slits between adjacent warps of your choice, preferably 1" away from either selvedge.

Weave at least 3" (7.5 cm.) of slits, shifting their positions at random in both directions. Create one slit that is at least 1½" (3.75 cm.) long. This slit will be sewn according to the directions in the technical advice. The others will be left open, for comparison.

The slit technique. Note the weft turns around adjacent warps.

Deleting two colors of weft yarns without mingling the two colors.

41

The process of sewing a slit from the front of the work. Note the slit in the tapestry, the blunt, curved needle, and the thread with an overhand knot and a long tail.

Attaching the sewing thread to a warp.

The sewing thread is securely attached to the tapestry, leaving a tail long enough to be pulled to the reverse side.

Tips & Advice

Sewing a slit. To experiment with sewing a slit, adjust the weaving space to position the longest slit between the front beam and the reed. The warp should be adjusted to its normal tension. Thread a blunt needle with about 20″ (50 cm.) of strong quilting thread, related in hue and value to one of the adjacent weft colors. Tie an overhand knot about 3″ above the two ends of the thread.

Begin sewing the slit at its lower edge. Use the tip of the needle to push aside the wefts around the warp to the right of the slit, then carry the needle around this warp and between the two threads, thus securing the sewing thread to the warp. Steer the tails of the sewing thread to the back of the tapestry, where they will be tied to other tails during the finishing process. Short, unsecured ends of thread have a tendency to protrude through the woven surface, months or even years later.

Push the wefts apart with the tip of the needle, to expose the warp on the left side of the slit. This warp, and the one around which you secured the sewing thread, will be the only two warps involved in closing the slit. Carry the point of the needle over this warp, around it, and upward through the slit. Then carry the point of the needle over the original warp, around it, and upward through the slit. You have created a figure eight around the two warps to either side of the slit.

Each figure eight should be planned to evenly advance the stitches toward the top of the slit, using the rows of weft as a guide. One complete stitch every fourth row should be sufficient. Slits that are very long or those in a tapestry to be mounted with the warps horizontal may need to be stitched every second row. Always bury the figure eights between rows of weft. Do not pull the stitches excessively; the objective is to butt the two colors invisibly, not to overlap or distort them.

To end the sewing, surround a warp twice; bring the needle up on one side of this warp and a long loop of the remaining sewing thread on the other side of the same warp. With the two long ends of the sewing thread, tie a secure, square knot around the warp. Use a crochet hook to draw the tails of the sewing thread to the back of the tapestry.

You can sew slits from either the right or the wrong side of the tapestry, even after the tapestry has been removed from the loom. However, the tension of the loom may be used to your advantage. If the warps are taut as you surround them with thread, there is less distortion of the contours. Also, when you stitch against a firm textile surface, the sewing proceeds more quickly. (Think about needlework held tightly between hoops.)

Warp direction. If a tapestry is mounted with the warp vertical, you may choose to sew the slits or not, depending only upon how unsewn slits might affect your design. Vertical slits cause few structural problems unless they are quite long. Even slits that are visibly open will not cause significant sagging or weakening of the textile. You may have designed a tapestry to take advantage of the clean contour lines possible only with slits. Or you may actually prefer the appearance of a series of slits as they open slightly, creating a secondary rhythm of gentle dimensional curves, similar to those in kilim textiles.

But if a tapestry is to be mounted with the weft vertical, any slits of ½″ (1.25 cm.) or longer should be securely sewn. Not only will they eventually become large gaps, causing the tapestry to sag unattractively, but the important structure of the textile may also be compromised, since the uneven distribution of weight produces stress along both sides of the slit.

As with all potential problems a tapestry weaver might anticipate, the larger and heavier the tapestry, the more troublesome the consequences.

Slits as selvedges. Slits are actually selvedges within the tapestry design and should be treated as such. As each successive weft reverses its direction around the relay warp, it should be stacked neatly over the previous weft. Do not exaggerate the slit by pulling the weft too tightly around the warp, and do not create sloppy or loopy slits by carrying the weft too loosely around the warp.

Placing slits. Slits may be planned into a design taking their structural weaknesses into consideration. For instance, you could frequently shift the positions of a slit or a series of slits to prevent any one of them from becoming overly long. Or you could shift a slit back and forth between two spaces, creating a series of short, staggered slits. The clever weavers who designed beautiful, tapestry-woven saddlebags for camels carefully planned slits corresponding to the curve of the camel's hump.

Complexities. The positions of the slits and the placement of the colors can be shifted only as two butterflies are woven toward each other. Experimenting freely as you weave this example will bring this home. When you weave an actual tapestry, however, you must place colors where the design dictates and, at the same time, consider the placement of any slits relative to the structure of the tapestry.

Slit Control During the Weaving Process

General Directions

Choose three colors of weft yarn with contrasting hues and values, and make a butterfly with each.

Into the next shed, enter the three butterflies, traveling in opposition to one another. Begin weaving this example in the same manner as the previous section—relaying three butterflies, while creating two slits.

When the slits become about ¼" (.6 cm.) long (about six or eight rows), shift the relays of the center butterfly, creating two small links. One link will connect the center area with the area to its right, and the other will connect the center area with the one to its left. In other words, as the center butterfly travels toward the left, shift its relay and the relay of the left butterfly one warp in that direction; then, as the center butterfly travels right, shift its relay and the relay of the right butterfly one warp in that direction.

Pay careful attention to the actions of the warps as you shift the relays of the center butterfly. If the new warp is raised as the center butterfly is woven toward it, weave under it in that shed; but if the new warp is lowered as the center butterfly is woven toward it, wait until the shed changes to weave around this warp. It makes no difference to the appearance of the link whether you execute it in one row or the other. Remember, it takes two rows of weaving to complete a pass. After you have woven the two links, return to the original relay positions, continuing the original two slits.

Weave 2" (5 cm.), linking the slits at regular intervals. Both slits will be 2" long, but their sides will be joined every ¼". Rest the butterflies in their present positions.

The first stitch.

The second stitch.

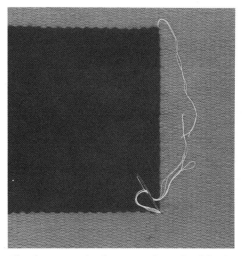

The slit is completely sewn. The tails of thread at both ends can be drawn to the reverse side. Photographed by George Goodwin.

Inserting an isolated locking weft across a slit.

Directly above the previous example and with the two slits in the same positions, experiment with another ancient technique for slit control. This time, the slits will be joined by an invisible locking weft traveling from selvedge to selvedge, on either a boat or a stick shuttle. First, wind your chosen shuttle with an extremely fine, soft yarn. Unmercerized, 20/2 cotton yarn works well as a locking weft. Sewing thread could also be used. Although this weft is not visible, I prefer to use an unobtrusive gray, of a value related to one of the three color areas.

Into the next shed, enter the locking weft at one selvedge in the usual manner. Weave it to the opposite selvedge and beat firmly. Then weave the three butterflies as usual, into the same shed as the locking weft, either meeting or relaying in the same positions. Change sheds and repeat the procedure: first the locking weft, then the three butterflies. Weave a 2″ example of this technique.

Tips & Advice

Linking techniques. The first method of slit-control will noticeably affect the appearance of the tapestry. The links are actually intrusions of one color into another's territory. Some tapestry weavers have cleverly managed to incorporate these obvious effects into their designs.

Contrast. The visual effects of woven links vary markedly with the yarns used. If two weft colors are closely related in hue and value, the links will not be quite as conspicuous. But if adjacent weft colors contrast sharply, woven links may become an important design element; they may even introduce an emphatic pattern along the edge of a slit.

Factors to consider. You, the weaver/designer, control the placement of these links. Some things to keep in mind are the number of links to be planned along a slit, the spacing of the links at regular or irregular intervals, the use of one or both weft colors for creating the links, and the effect of these choices on the design.

Variations of the locking weft. In the second method of slit control, the locking weft was woven first at every change of shed, and the tapestry weft followed in the same shed. This is one of the least visible methods for weaving a locking weft, but there are other variations. It is also possible to weave two picks of locking weft between each pick of tapestry weft, changing sheds after every pick. Depending upon the weight or the softness of the thread, the locking weft may appear as very fine lines between the picks of tapestry weft. It will certainly result in a lighter weight tapestry with a considerably coarser texture. The advantages are that all slits are securely locked, and that fewer rows of weaving are required to make the tapestry.

You can also weave the locking weft every second or third row, carrying the tapestry weft around the thread at the selvedge. Don't begin weaving an entire tapestry in this technique without a great deal of experimentation. As you sample the locking weft variations, observe their distinctive textures. Compare the appearance of a tapestry surface woven with this technique to that of other techniques. When the sampler is removed from the loom, observe the lighter weight of this example.

Drawbacks. One disadvantage of locking wefts is that the tapestry must be woven in complete rows, one at a time. As we proceed through this tapestry sampler, you will learn weaving techniques and approaches to design interpretation that may entice you away from weaving row by row.

Since I believe that students should learn tapestry weaving on a small scale, by focusing on only a few butterflies executing similar tasks, this sampler is narrow and, for the most part, woven row by row, allowing you to concentrate on each technique and its color effects. However, all of the techniques you have learned so far, and most of those yet to come, could be used in building vertical segments of a design. You may discover, as have many others, that you prefer this manner of interpreting your designs. If so, you will need to choose another method of slit control.

Bubbling. Do not bubble the locking weft. Lay it into the shed at a slight upward angle, then beat firmly. An excess of this weft will appear unattractively on the surface of the tapestry, along the bottom of each row of tapestry weft.

Exposed warps. Used with the warp/weft proportions specified earlier, the locking-weft technique should not cause exposed warps on your sampler. However, there are always individual variables that may result in either exposed warps or exposed locking wefts. If this is the case, reduce the size of your butterfly to four or even three strands.

Another variation. Tapestry weavers who prefer to build certain elements of the design individually, rather than weaving from selvedge to selvedge every row, should try this technique for inserting an isolated locking weft across a slit: Cut a 10″ (25 cm.) length of the fine, soft thread used as the locking weft. Open the shed opposite the last row of tapestry weaving, and lay the locking weft into the shed for about 2″, straddling the slit evenly. Draw the two ends of the locking weft upward, out of the shed. Beat and change sheds. Weave the two ends of the locking weft back into this shed, toward each other. Overlap their tails over two or three lowered warps, and drop them to the back of the tapestry. The tails will be tied to one another during the finishing process. Beat and change sheds again for the next row of tapestry weaving. You have invisibly closed the slit at that point. The subsequent rows of tapestry weft will pack to cover the two short rows of thread. This isolated locking weft may be used as needed, about every fourth or sixth row at most.

Dovetail Technique

General Directions

A series of single dovetails.

Choose two colors of weft yarn with a very high degree of contrast, and make a butterfly with each.

Enter the two butterflies into the next weaving shed, one at each selvedge, converging near the center of the row. At this point, the butterflies should emerge from between two adjacent raised warps. Change sheds. Weave the butterflies back to the selvedges, reversing the directions of both butterflies around the raised warp between them. This creates a single dovetail connection at the juncture of the two weft colors. Build an orderly series of dovetails, consistently carrying one of the weft colors first around the common warp. Weave about 1″ in this manner, ending the example with the two butterflies resting at the selvedges. Observe the secure connection between the two weft colors, the sawtooth appearance of the vertical line, and the slight ridge along the dovetail warp.

45

A series of double dovetails.

A series of triple dovetails.

A series of triple-dovetail variations.

The second example creates a single dovetail around a raised warp as the two butterflies meet. Open the shed for the next row of weaving, and choose any raised warp to be used for the next dovetail. Weave the butterfly at the left to the dovetail warp and under it; then weave the butterfly at the right to the dovetail warp and under it. The two wefts have crossed under the common warp. Change sheds and weave both butterflies back to the selvedges. For the return trip to the selvedges, either butterfly may be woven first, but be consistent about the placement of the two colors around the dovetail warp. A single dovetail connection has now been created around this common warp in essentially the same manner as the first example. Weave 1″ of this dovetail technique, then rest the butterflies at the selvedges.

Observe the identical appearances of the two single dovetail examples, demonstrating similar but inverted techniques. Note also that it is possible to dovetail two converging wefts around any warp, whether it is raised in the shed as the butterflies meet, or in the shed as they separate.

The next variation is a double dovetail. Open the shed for the next row of weaving, and choose any raised warp for the position of the dovetail. Weave one of the butterflies to this warp. Change sheds and weave the same butterfly back to the selvedge. Repeat this procedure for a total of four picks with the same butterfly. Next, weave four picks with the other butterfly, reversing its direction twice around the same dovetail warp. These eight picks complete the double dovetail. Weave 1½″ of this example, ending with the butterflies resting at the selvedges. Look closely at two important effects: a pronounced series of notches between the two weft colors, and much less of a ridge along the common warp.

The next variation is a triple dovetail. Open the shed for the next row of weaving, and choose a different dovetail warp. This time, weave six picks at a time around the dovetail warp with each color of weft yarn, a total of 12 picks per triple dovetail. Weave about 1½″ of the triple dovetail, and again end with the two butterflies resting at the selvedges.

This time, examine the large, emphatic notches between the two weft colors. You may also notice a slight spreading of the warps to either side of the dovetail.

Move the dovetail position one more time, and again weave a series of triple dovetails. This time, the example is a triple dovetail variation. Weave six rows with each weft color as follows:

Rows one and two: Weave to the dovetail warp, around it, and back to the selvedge.

Rows three and four: Weave toward the dovetail warp, stopping short of it by one warp. Relay around the warp adjacent to the dovetail warp and back to the selvedge.

Rows five and six: Weave to the dovetail warp, around it, and back to the selvedge.

Repeat this procedure, alternating the two colors. Weave about 2″ of the triple dovetail variation. End both butterflies at the selvedges. Observe that by avoiding the common warp with rows three and four of each weft color, you have created a sharply pointed and secure dovetail, similar in scale to the first triple dovetail, but with less distortion of the surrounding weave.

Tips & Advice

Superior strength. The strength of this weft-crossing technique is superior to any other. For one thing, a warp is involved in every dovetail. The warp, a very strong yarn that runs evenly and continuously through the weave, forms the substructure of the tapestry and the dominant element of every interlacing. Moreover, two wefts surround the warp securely from opposite directions. A tapestry with dovetailed connections can be mounted with either the warp or the weft vertical, with no stress or sagging along contour lines. For rugs and other tapestry-woven articles that must be even more durable, the dovetail is the most appropriate technique for joining adjacent weft colors.

Disadvantages. There are three potential disadvantages to this technique, all of which are matters of personal preference.

First, two weft colors occupy the same warp at the dovetail, creating small, medium, or large notches, depending upon whether you have used single, double, or triple dovetails. The sett will also be a factor in determining the size of these notches. In general, the more widely spaced the warp, the more emphatic the notches. Whatever their scale, these distinctive sawtooth vertical lines can be incorporated into the design, or they can be regarded as idiomatic of this technique.

Second, the warps spread around the dovetail, especially triple dovetails. Turning the weft firmly around the dovetail warp should minimize this distortion, but using the triple dovetail variation will provide even better results.

Third, a slight ridge develops along the dovetail warp, as a result of relaying two wefts around the same warp for several rows in succession. To eliminate this ridge, shift the position of the dovetail at regular intervals, redistributing the excess weft laterally. Or dovetail the wefts intermittently, every third or fourth pass.

Firm turns. Pull the wefts firmly around the common warp, more firmly perhaps than with any other technique. This will ensure a neat, flat dovetail.

Consistent color. All dovetails involve two colors of yarn and one warp; therefore, when approaching the common warp, always carry the same color around it first.

Dovetailing a solid-color background. The simple dovetail can be pulled into service to assist with another tapestry technicality: weaving with several butterflies, relaying at random to create a solid-color background (see Chapter One). By dovetailing converging wefts, you eliminate those annoying tiny slits and most of the texture associated with solid-color relays; you also create a very sturdy, tightly woven background with a smooth surface. And by carefully distributing the positions of the dovetails, you avoid any visible evidence of the actions of the multiple butterflies.

Dovetails are especially useful when relaying solid-color multiple wefts across a narrow area, such as the bottom of a triangle or a circle. The starting point of such shapes provides too few warps upon which to relay two butterflies without creating a slit. However, the position of a dovetail can be shifted invisibly back and forth between as few as two warps. And tiny, complicated areas of a tapestry seem to gain strength and stability from dovetail crossings.

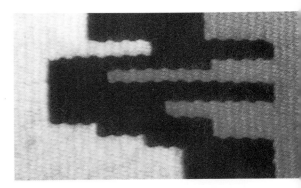

The photographs on this page and on page 49 illustrate the weft relays and crossings described in the text. Above: basic slit technique.

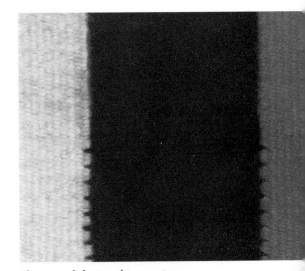

Slit control during the weaving process.

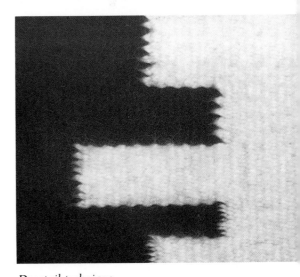

Dovetail technique.

Two opposing wefts meeting between two adjacent raised warps.

The active weft carried under and around the passive weft, under the common raised warp, and through the shed.

The final step of the single weft interlock: weaving the passive butterfly through the shed.

Single Weft Interlock
General Directions

Choose two colors of weft yarn, contrasting strongly in both hue and value to emphasize the visual characteristics of this crossing technique. Make a butterfly with each of these weft yarns.

Enter both butterflies into the next shed, one at either selvedge. Weave them toward each other to meet at some point near the center of the row.

Change sheds. This is the point at which the two butterflies will be interlocked—where you reverse their directions to return them to the selvedges. First, carry the darker butterfly under and around the yarn of the lighter one, under the raised warp between the two butterflies, and into the shed to be woven back to the selvedge. Then, having been interlocked, the lighter butterfly can be woven to the opposite selvedge. Bubble and beat the row.

Change sheds, and weave the two butterflies to the same position again. Change sheds and interlock them in the same manner as before. Practice weaving neat, consistent interlocks in this position for about 1″. Complete at least eight interlocks, stacked neatly one above the other. Keep in mind that no special manipulation should occur in the shed as the two butterflies meet. The interlock is always executed in the shed as the butterflies travel toward the selvedges. Be consistent about first carrying the darker butterfly under and around the yarn of the lighter butterfly, then under the raised warp and into the shed. Rest the butterflies at the selvedges, and examine the sawtooth vertical line.

Shift the position of the interlock by weaving the two butterflies to meet between a different pair of raised warps. (Move at least 1″ in either direction away from the previous interlock.) Since it would be possible to interlock between any two warps, there are as many interlocking positions along a row of weaving as there are spaces between warps. Practice interlocking in this new position for about 1″.

Next, practice moving the interlock one position at a time to the right, forming a diagonal line between the two colors. Carefully consider the placement of each interlock as the butterflies meet, and again as they separate. The meeting place does not necessarily change each time the butterflies converge, for there are two interlocking positions between every pair of raised warps. One interlocking position is in the space between the raised warp at the left and the lowered warp, and the other is between the raised warp at the right and the lowered warp. These two positions become even more obvious as the shed is changed. Use both of these spaces as you regularly shift the interlock one space to the right, every other row.

As you proceed with these constantly shifting interlocks, observe the common raised warp between the converging butterflies. One of the butterflies must be carried under the raised warp as it returns to its selvedge. And as it is this butterfly that always takes the active part of the interlocking procedure, it should be woven first. Be sure to carry this active butterfly under and around the yarn of the passive butterfly before it travels under the raised warp and through the shed. Since you will be shifting the interlock one position to the right each time, you should alternate the two butterflies as active butterflies. Weave about 1½″ of this example, creating a low diagonal line between the two weft colors.

Reverse the direction of the diagonal line to practice shifting the position of the interlock to the left. If the interlock is moved two spaces every other row, the same weft color is used actively at each interlock, resulting in a smooth diagonal line. You may also wish to try moving the interlock around at random, following an imaginary line. Or, introduce a third butterfly. In this case, the center butterfly and the butterfly at the right will meet in one shed; in the alternate sheds, the center butterfly and the butterfly at the left will meet. As the wefts converge, establish their interlocking position and, as you reverse their directions, interlock them. In each row, one pair of butterflies will interlock and the other will meet.

Observe the ease with which this crossing technique can be introduced between pairs of opposing wefts in any position.

Tips & Advice

Design considerations. By carrying the active butterfly (the butterfly designated to travel under the common raised warp) under and around the yarn of the passive butterfly, you create a single weft interlock in the neatest, most consistent manner. Interpreting an actual tapestry cartoon (a design painted or drawn to full scale) requires constant decisions as to which weft should be carried under the common raised warp, according to the placement of the weft colors in the design.

Taut turns. Interlocks may appear sloppy or lumpy if the weft yarns are not pulled taut as they reverse their directions. Excess weft may even bulge unattractively from the surface of the tapestry. After the active butterfly has been interlocked and woven through the shed, tighten the interlock by tugging gently but firmly on both butterflies. The common raised warp will offer some necessary resistance against this tugging. Then, as the passive butterfly is woven through the shed, pack the interlock against the previous row of weaving with your finger. Bubble the weft across the row of weaving without involving the area of the interlock.

Interlocking and slit technique. Compare the slightly bulky, sawtooth line of the interlocks with the sharp color contrasts and flat edges of the slit technique. When choosing a technique for handling discontinous wefts, consider the stability of the woven structure as well as any visual effects. Perhaps you would prefer to combine interlocking and slit techniques along the curve of a contour line. Or interlock every third or fourth pass—as often as required to control a slit. Or play up the unique and obviously handwoven look of the interlock. Interlocking every edge of every color area could lend a subtle technical unity to a tapestry design.

Warp and weft. As with all weft crossings, the proportions of warp and weft affect the appearance of the interlocks. Fine, soft, regularly spun weft yarns can be securely interlocked in a neat, inconspicuous manner. Of course, a weft of this weight must be used with a fine, closely spaced warp. Conversely, interlocks created with heavy, coarse, kinky, or unevenly spun weft yarns are inevitably lumpy and obtrusive, especially if a series is stacked vertically.

The value of the technique. By interlocking adjacent wefts, you build a strong and stabile textile and, at the same time, efficiently place colors in their correct positions according to the design. The easiest way to accomplish both of these important tasks is to weave with butterflies traveling in opposite directions. By doing so, you can interlock two or 20 butterflies across a row of weaving, conveniently shifting around colors at will. To skillfully handle more than two butterflies at a time, simply remember that converging pairs of butterflies meet every other row. In the alternate rows, these same pairs are interlocked and woven away from each other, to meet other butterflies or to travel toward a selvedge.

Single weft interlock.

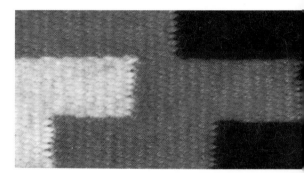

Rolakan interlock.

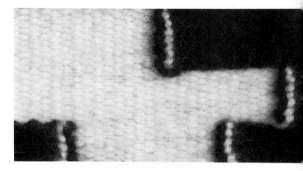

Double weft interlock (wrong side).

Summary:

The Single Weft Interlock

1. There is a potential interlocking position between every two warps along the entire width of a tapestry.
2. By weaving with wefts traveling in opposite directions, you have the flexibility to shift an interlock to any of these positions.
3. Opposing wefts meet between adjacent raised warps, providing at this point two possible positions for interlocking.
4. As the shed is changed for the wefts to reverse their directions, the interlock can be executed to either the left or the right of the raised warp between the wefts.
5. Either weft can be carried under the raised warp as they interlock.
6. The decision as to which weft should be carried under the raised warp will depend upon which color of weft should be placed in that area according to the tapestry design.
7. The weft designated to be woven under the raised warp at the interlock is the active weft.
8. To execute a single weft interlock, first carry the active weft under and around the yarn of the passive weft and into the shed. Then weave the passive weft through the shed.

Eighth-century Coptic tapestry, slit and triple-dovetailed, eccentric wefts. Collection of the Textile Museum, Washington, D.C.

Rolakan Interlock

General Directions

Choose three colors of weft yarn, contrasting with each other in hue and value, and make a butterfly with each.

Enter all three butterflies into the next shed. The first butterfly should be entered at the left selvedge and woven toward the right for about 3″ where it will emerge from between two raised warps. The second butterfly should be entered around the lowered warp to the right of the emerging first butterfly, also to be woven toward the right for about 3″. The third butterfly should be entered around the lowered warp to the right of the emerging second butterfly and woven to the right selvedge. Observe the six boundaries of the three colors of weft yarns: the two raised warps to the left of the emerging first and second butterflies, the two lowered warps around which the second and third butterflies were entered, and the two selvedges. The butterflies will be interlocked in the spaces between the warps that form these boundaries.

The weft at the selvedge being crossed over the weft waiting to be woven next.

Begin weaving each row with the butterfly at the selvedge—in this case, the right selvedge. As you weave the first butterfly to meet the second, cross the yarn of the butterfly that has been woven over the yarn of the butterfly waiting to be woven. Weave the second butterfly to meet the third. Again, cross the yarn of the butterfly that has been woven over the yarn of the butterfly waiting to be woven. Weave the third butterfly to the left selvedge.

The second weft being woven through the shed after the crossing.

The next row will be woven beginning, as always, with the butterfly at the selvedge. However, in this row, no interlocking occurs; the butterflies are simply woven to their boundaries. The Rolakan interlock is similar to the single weft interlock in that a crossing occurs every other row. Therefore, because the wefts were interlocked in row two, they should also be interlocked in rows four, six, and eight—not in rows three, five, and seven. A better way to remember the interlocking shed is to relate it to the weaving direction. For instance, in this example the interlocking takes place as you weave from right to left; if you are weaving from left to right, no interlocking takes place. Either shed (either direction) may be used for interlocking, but to keep the line between the colors neat and regular, be consistent.

Weave for about 1″, practicing the Rolakan technique and creating two neat stacks of interlocks. Then shift the positions of both interlocks 1″ to the right—possible only as the butterflies travel from left to right. To move the interlocks, reverse the usual order of weaving. First, weave the butterfly at the right to the right selvedge and beat the row. Then weave the middle butterfly across its color area and into the color area of the weft to its right. It should emerge from the shed 1″ to the right of the previous interlock. Again, beat the row. For 1″ there will be two wefts in the shed. Notice the new interlocking position which has been established by the action of the middle butterfly.

The usual method of shifting a Rolakan interlock: carrying both wefts through the shed from the same direction.

Shift the position of the other interlock in the same manner. Weave the butterfly at the left selvedge to a new interlocking position, 1″ to the right of its right boundary. As this weft color is shifted, it too will introduce double weft into the shed for 1″. Beat again and change sheds.

By weaving this row, you have established two different interlocking positions. Begin again to interlock regularly in these new positions as the butterflies travel from right to left. Weave several rows, then shift the interlocks to the left—possible only as you weave the butterflies from right to left.

Normally, rows woven from right to left would be interlocking rows, to keep the appearance of the interlocks consistent. However, it is impossible to interlock and shift positions in the same row. Therefore, without interlocking, weave the butterfly at the left to the left selvedge; weave the middle butterfly to a new interlocking position, 2″ to the left of its left boundary; and weave the butterfly at the right to a new interlocking position, 2″ to the left of its left boundary.

Shifting the interlocks to the left will result in a total of three rows with no interlocks: the row woven from left to right, following the previous interlock; the row woven from right to left, establishing different interlocking positions; and another row woven from left to right. Skipping an occasional interlock in order to shift colors causes no structural or visual problems. After this break in the routine, begin again to interlock consistently each time the butterflies travel from right to left.

Weave several rows with the interlocks in the new positions. End the weaving of this example in the shed with no interlocking. End two of the butterflies at their interior boundaries and the third at a selvedge.

Tips & Advice

Rolakan and single weft. The Rolakan interlock looks much like the single weft interlock. Perhaps the Rolakan interlocks are a bit bulkier, because you cannot tighten the two wefts against each other at the same time, and there may be a bit more spreading of the warps to either side of the interlock for the same reason. But the sawtooth line between the two colors is identical.

Starting a row. Unless you are shifting the position of an interlock, begin weaving every row with the butterfly at the selvedge. Then the last butterfly to be woven in any row will be conveniently in your hand to be woven first in the next row.

Tightening the lock. The sheds in which you do not interlock provide the perfect opportunity for refining the appearance of the weft crossing. As you pick up each butterfly to weave it to its next position, tug slightly on the interlock, eliminating any lumpy excess of weft.

Applications. On many occasions, you may find it useful to know how to interlock wefts traveling in the same direction. Perhaps you prefer weaving tapestries row by row, from one selvedge to the other. In that case, you may find it easier to add or delete weft colors if the butterflies are all traveling and interlocking in the same direction. Even if you usually weave with opposing butterflies, there may be times when a certain butterfly, especially one newly introduced, must be woven for a few rows in the same direction as its neighbor. Or maybe you need to begin organizing your butterflies for a double weft interlock, described in the next section. At these times, the Rolakan technique can be drafted into service.

Alternative shift. Rolakan interlocks are less complicated to execute than single weft interlocks, especially if you are weaving a series of them, one complete row at a time. However, they cannot always be shifted as neatly or efficiently. For instance, in my example I had no exposed warps as a result of shifting the interlocks according to the directions. But I used a very soft weft, and my loom provided excellent tension, two important factors influencing the packing of the weft. Even slight variations in the quality and weight of the weft yarns, the tension of the warp, or the size and weight of the loom could prevent the double weft from packing closely enough to completely cover the warp.

If your warps are exposed, use an alternative method for shifting the positions of Rolakan interlocks. To shift to the right, weave the butterfly at the right to the right selvedge; weave the middle butterfly across its present color area to the opposite boundary; drop it through the warps to the back of the tapestry; and bring it to the surface again in the new position. A loop of weft yarn will travel across the reverse side of the tapestry. Repeat the procedure with the butterfly at the left. You have shifted the interlocking positions without changing the directions of the butterflies or doubling the weft in the shed. A shift to the left can be executed in the same manner.

Nordic treasures. Generations of Scandinavian weavers have used the Rolakan interlock to build handsome tapestry-technique rugs. Their choice of warp has traditionally been a heavy, tightly spun linen, doubled or tripled and spaced widely in the reed. Interlaced with this warp are several strands of heavy, tightly spun wool or wool/cowhair blends. These materials yield a rug that is very warm and nearly indestructible. And, as the carefully planned proportions forgive a bit of extra weft in the shed, the rugs are completely reversible; interlocks can be shifted around invisibly at the weaver's discretion, and weft tails can be concealed in the shed.

In addition, the rugs are woven on sturdy horizontal looms. Each row is woven completely from one selvedge to the other, then beaten very firmly against the previous row. Tightly packed wefts do not shift underfoot, abrading one another.

But the distinguishing characteristic of these Nordic treasures is their complicated and ingeniously blended colors of yarn, yarns carefully selected and twisted together as they are carried through the shed. This unique design element is possible only if the proportions of warp and weft allow the thickness of several strands of weft in a single butterfly. This time-honored skill of blending more than one color of weft yarn in a shed will be explained in Chapter Five. But the lesson here is very definitely the interdependency of technique, design, the use of color, and the structure of the textile.

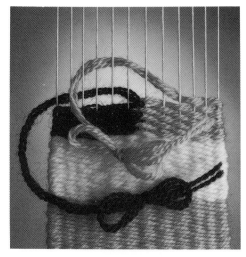

The author's alternative method of shifting a Rolakan interlock: floating one of the weft colors across the back of the tapestry.

The first row of the double weft interlock.

Double Weft Interlock

General Directions

This ingenious interlock was brought to my attention by Peter Collingwood in *The Techniques of Rug Weaving* (see the bibliography). No tapestry weaver should be without this method of creating perfectly delineated vertical lines of any width, potentially as narrow as a single warp. This technique does have three limitations: It must be executed from the back of the tapestry; it results in a textile that is not reversible; and all wefts involved with a double weft interlock must be traveling in the same direction. Thus, the side of the example facing you will be the wrong side of the double weft interlock—a thick ridge comprised of vertical rows of both colors of weft yarns. With a mirror, you can see the right side of the interlock on the reverse side of the example—a flat, straight line between the two weft colors.

Choose two colors of weft yarn with contrasting hues and values, and make a butterfly with each.

Into the next shed, enter both butterflies traveling from left to right. One butterfly should be entered at the left selvedge and woven toward the right for about 4″ (10 cm.), where it will emerge from between two raised warps. The second butterfly should be entered around the lowered warp to the right of the emerging first butterfly and woven to the right selvedge. The double weft interlock will be created in the space between the raised warp to the left of the emerging butterfly and the lowered warp to its right.

As with the Rolakan interlock, begin weaving each row with the butterfly at the selvedge; weave the butterfly at the right selvedge to meet the emerging butterfly. Cross the butterfly that has been woven over the butterfly waiting to be woven. Weave the remaining butterfly to the left selvedge and change sheds. Then weave the butterfly at the left selvedge to meet the emerging butterfly, and again cross the butterfly that has been woven over the waiting one. Weave the remaining butterfly to the right selvedge. As indicated by its name, the double weft interlock requires interlocking in every row. This double crossing action forces the excess weft to the working side of the tapestry, while creating a sharp vertical line on the opposite side.

Weave at least 1″ with the double weft interlock. End the example with one butterfly at the right selvedge and the other emerging at the interlock.

In the next row of weaving, shift the position of the interlock at least 1″ to the left, in the same manner as the Rolakan interlock: Either place double weft into the shed as you weave the butterfly at the right to the new interlocking position, or carry it across the back of the tapestry to its new interlocking position. Remember, in this case it is the back of the tapestry that is facing you. Weave another 1″ with the interlock in this position. End the example with one butterfly at the left selvedge and the other emerging at the interlock.

The next experiment involves creating a very fine vertical line along a single warp. Double weft interlocks executed between the vertical line and the adjacent background wefts result in clean lines and maintain the structural quality of the tapestry. Choose a third contrasting color of weft yarn and make a butterfly.

First, shift the position of the double weft interlock at least 1″ to the right, using either of the two previously explained procedures (introducing double weft into the shed, or looping weft across the back of the tapestry).

The second row of the double weft interlock.

Then change sheds and weave the butterfly at the right selvedge toward the emerging butterfly. In this case, the two butterflies will not meet between adjacent raised warps. They should be closely situated, but in a manner positioning one raised warp and one lowered warp between them. Enter the third butterfly traveling toward the left by wrapping its tail around the raised warp between the two original butterflies. Weave the remaining butterfly to the left selvedge. Note that no interlocking occurred as you shifted the position of the interlock or as you introduced the third butterfly.

With a permanent marker, place a mark on the warp around which the third butterfly was entered—the position of the vertical line. The newly entered butterfly will be woven around this warp every other row, and interlocked in every row with both adjacent butterflies.

Begin to interlock the three butterflies in the next row, as you weave from left to right. Observe that in this row the marked warp is lowered, inaccessible to the center butterfly. Do not try to weave the center butterfly in this row, but interlock it at both sides to maintain a consistent visual effect and to correctly position all three butterflies for weaving and interlocking in the next row. In other words, weave the butterfly at the left selvedge through the shed and carry its yarn over the yarn of the center butterfly. Float the yarn of the center butterfly over the marked warp, and carry it over the yarn of the third butterfly. Weave the third butterfly to the right selvedge. In the next row, follow this procedure in reverse, with the exception of the center butterfly, which should be woven under the raised, marked warp.

Weave at least 1″ of this narrow, contrasting vertical line, checking its right side frequently with a mirror. The bulky, fragmented ridges facing you will seem unrelated to the neat, flat, sharply defined line on the reverse side. You may wish to practice shifting the line in both directions, over several warps, or one warp at a time. End the three butterflies, carefully keeping the colors within their respective boundaries.

Tips & Advice

Reverse side. Although the right side of this interlock appears on the reverse side of the example, you will probably prefer to retain the continuity of the tapestry sampler by securing all weft tails on the reverse side, as usual. If you used this technique on an actual tapestry, you would have to weave the entire tapestry from the reverse side. Then the reverse side of the double weft interlock and all weft tails would face you. However, this is the only upside-down technique on your sampler, and after it is removed from the loom, you will have a unified right side and access to both sides of the double weft interlock for future reference.

Tightening the lock. The double weft interlock should be tightened and refined in the same manner as the Rolakan interlock: Tug gently at the interlock as you reverse the direction of each butterfly. Check the stacks of contrasting colors at the position of the interlock. If these lines appear straight and even, the line on the front of the tapestry will correspond.

Visibility. Double weft interlocks, like single interlocks, are executed in the spaces between warps. In this case, however, the thick, prominent ridge of weft yarn on the weaving surface may block your view. At each interlock, check both the crossing and the weaving to be sure that the interlock occurs in the correct space and that the colors are confined to their boundaries.

The front side of a double-weft interlock, the finest possible woven line without slits. Photographed by George Goodwin.

Shifts. Shift the position of the double weft interlock in the same manner as the Rolakan interlock: Shift to the right as you weave the butterflies to the right, and shift to the left as you weave the butterflies to the left. Either place double weft into the shed, or loop the weft across the back of the tapestry as a new position is established.

Neatness. It may seem unlikely that this more complicated procedure could result in the neatest of all possible interlocks. But by crossing the wefts twice, then forcing the resulting lump of tightly interlocked yarn to the working side of the tapestry, you keep the right side clear of clutter. On the other hand, the single interlocks occur squarely in the spaces between warps, appearing much the same from both sides of a tapestry.

Visual continuity. Creating a narrow vertical line involves weaving a contrasting weft under a single warp, every other row (the row in which that warp is raised). In the alternate rows, the contrasting weft cannot be woven; it floats over the assigned warp. However, it must be interlocked with both adjacent butterflies in every row. This ensures visual continuity, and the correct positions of all butterflies for subsequent weaving and interlocking.

Variations in texture. The texture of a narrow, double-interlocked vertical line appears on the right side of the tapestry as a stack of horizontal stitches—slightly different from the texture of the surrounding weave. This is a result of carrying the isolated weft around the designated warp from only one direction, every other row. The minute variations in density and texture are neither obtrusive nor objectionable, and the warp is completely covered. You may even prefer this slight inconsistency, especially if your inserted vertical line is describing letters. However, if you wish to approximate the adjacent texture more closely and, at the same time, compensate for having skipped this warp every other row, carry the weft a second time around the designated warp after the butterfly has been woven under it. This extra wrap creates a more firmly woven line with a texture similar to the surrounding weave. Experiment with both possibilities, compare the effects, and choose the method you prefer.

Shifting vertical lines. You can easily shift narrow vertical lines over a single warp in either direction. Simply carry the shifting weft over the adjacent weft in the same shed. Double weft in a shed over such a short distance should not cause exposed warps. Moving narrow lines in this manner is especially useful for inserting woven initials or calligraphic letters into a tapestry, a process that requires frequent shifting in both directions.

Applications. A technique that allows you to weave narrow vertical lines securely interlocked along both edges opens up numerous possibilities. Words, letters, or your initials can be described in this manner. Or a design can include fine vertical lines that would compromise the structure of the tapestry if they were woven with the slit technique. Perhaps a crucial contour would benefit from a contrasting vertical outline. If there is a need for any of these elements and the tapestry is being woven from the back, the double weft interlock can be successfully employed.

Joyce Hulbert, Untitled. Cotton warp; hand-dyed wool, silk, and linen weft; 36″ x 36″ (90 by 90 cm.); 1987. Hachures, double weft interlock.

Trudi Eldridge, Lyrical Landscape. Woven by Tapus Studio (Christine Laffer, interpretation; Ann Zerman Sanders, weaver); wool warp and weft; 22½″ x 37″ (56 by 93 cm.); 1989.

WEFT RELAYS AND CROSSINGS

Soyoo Hyunjoo Park, Kiting. Cotton, flax, polyester materials; 46″ x 57″ (115 by 143 cm.); 1987. Photo: George Mauro. Slit technique.

WEFT RELAYS AND CROSSINGS   58

*Margaretta Grandin Nettles,
Unicorn Tapestry (detail).
Linen warp, wool and silk
weft; 12″ x 23″ (30 by 58 cm.);
1974. Photo: Jack Weinhold.*

*Jan Yoors, Adoration of the
Golden Calf. Woven by Anna-
bert, Marianne, and Jan Yoors.
Cotton warp, wool weft; 9′ x
12′ (2.7 by 3.7 m.); 1957.
Photo: George Cserna. Collec-
tion of Mr. and Mrs. Hugo
Schwartz.*

*Rita Adrianou, Windmill. Cotton warp,
hand-spun singles wool weft; 9″ x 5″ (23 by 13
cm.); ca. 1986. Photo: Carmelina Margaret
D'Amelio. Collection of the author.*

Carol K. Russell, Directions. Fiskgarn/matt-varp warp; Persian wool, rayon, and silk wefts (black Fiskgarn/mattvarp as locking weft); 58" x 58" (145 by 145 cm.); 1987. Photo: George Mauro. Slit tapestry with shuttled locking weft.

*Christine Laffer, Pacific Stock Exchange.
Cotton warp, three-strand crewel yarn weft;
62" x 115" (155 by 288 cm.); 1983-85.*

*Jan Yoors, New York Skyline. Woven by
Annabert and Marianne Yoors. Cotton warp,
wool weft; 9' x 12' (2.7 by 3.7 m.); 1962.
Photo: George Cserna.*

WEFT RELAYS AND CROSSINGS

Turkish Cradle. Cotton warp, single-spun wool weft; 15″ x 52″ (38 by 130 cm.). Photo: George Mauro. Collection of Jason Nazmiyal/Rug & Kilim. Kilim technique (short slits, shifted laterally), geometric outlining on two warps, borders of soumak and twining.

Camel Bag from Iran. Two-ply wool warp, very fine single-spun wool weft; 56″ x 34″ (140 by 85 cm.). Photo: George Mauro. Collection of Jason Nazmiyal/Rug & Kilim. Functional slits: jute loops drawn through slits close the top of the bag, and a stick can be threaded through the loops for carrying it.

WEFT RELAYS AND CROSSINGS

Navajo Rug, Storm Pattern. Wool warp and weft; 34″ x 62″ (85 by 155 cm.). Photo: George Mauro. Collection of Carol and Ken Hopper. Rolakan-type interlocks, lazy lines, precise diagonal lines, serrated diagonal lines.

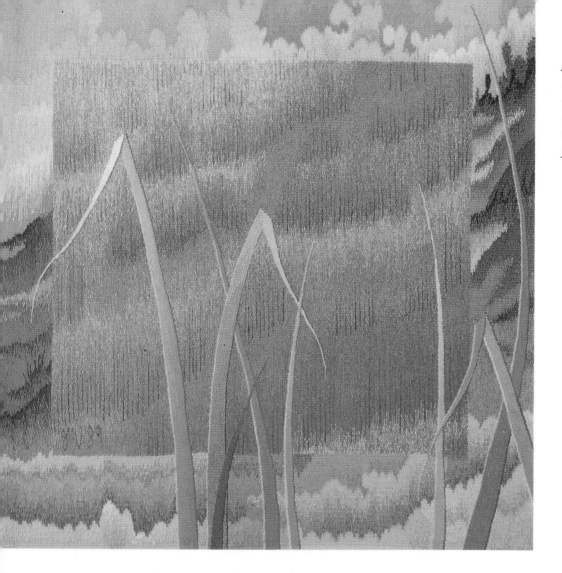

Julia Mitchell, Hills of Grass. Linen warp, wool weft; 38″ x 38″ (95 by 95 cm.); 1989. Photo: Bruno Debas. Single interlock, eccentric wefts (in foreground grasses).

Rojane Lamego, Tecelagem IX. Jute warp; jute, dyed jute, cotton, synthetic yarn, and remnant wefts; 31″ x 32″ (77 by 80 cm.); 1982. Photo: Wendy Shaull. Dovetail technique.

WEFT RELAYS AND CROSSINGS   64

Barbara Heller, Natan in Egypt (detail). *Linen warp, wool weft, some hand-spun, all hand-dyed; 59" x 48" (148 by 120 cm.); 1988. Photo: Barbara Cohen.*

Julia Mitchell, Boulders in a Windy Field. *Linen warp, wool weft; 66" x 28" (165 by 70 cm.); 1981. Eccentric wefts, no interlock, transparent top and bottom borders.*

Margaretta Grandin Nettles, Summer Field. *Linen warp, wool weft; 11' x 21' (3.4 by 6.4 m.); 1985. Photo: Jack Weinhold. Collection of Ann Charlotte Kranz.*

Susan Hart Henegar, The Working Girl Series: Sunday Morning. *Cotton warp, wool, cotton weft; 42″ x 54″ (105 by 135 cm.); 1990.*

Micala Sidore, Blues for Peter Stein. *Wool warp and weft; 30½″ x 41″ (76 by 103 cm.); 1989. Collection of Peter Stein.*

Vertical Lines

As you continue to broaden your exposure to the world of tapestry, either at shows or by looking at illustrations in books and magazines, you should begin to recognize many of the techniques included in your own sampler. You should also begin to look at tapestries from the perspective of the weaver—which is not necessarily the same as that of the viewer.

To determine whether a tapestry has been woven horizontally or vertically, look for the characteristic parallel ridges indicating the direction of the warps. These ridges are quite obvious, even in most photographs. Then, having identified the warps, you can recognize and evaluate the techniques the weaver chose for developing the vertical lines—vertical, that is, from the weaver's point of view.

To interpret a tapestry design effectively, a weaver must be able to create curved or diagonal lines between weft colors. A cartoon may include rigid diagonal lines expressing directions and energies important to the design. Or a human figure may require sensuous, curving contours traveling vertically or diagonally through the tapestry.

Because a line in a tapestry can be woven most efficiently with a horizontal or slightly oblique stroke of weft yarn, it would be logical to plan to weave from whichever direction (horizontal or vertical) prescribes the fewest vertical lines. You may be limited, however, by the width of your loom, or your design may contain many lines of various angles, creating equal problems in both directions. Thus, you need to be able to interpret all types of vertical lines.

Diagonal Lines

General Directions

Choose two colors of weft yarn with contrasting hues and values, and make a butterfly with each.

Enter the two butterflies into the next shed at the selvedges, placing the darker color to the right. Weave the butterflies toward each other, to meet at a point about 2″ (5 cm.) from the left selvedge. Change sheds. Reverse the directions of the butterflies around adjacent warps and weave them back to their respective selvedges. The first diagonal line, pointing upward and to the right, will originate from this first relay. The width of the lighter area at the left will be gradually increased by being shifted toward the right selvedge two warps every two rows, while the width of the darker area at the right will be concurrently decreased by being shifted in the same direction, by the same amount, and in the same number of rows.

Open the next weaving shed and observe the previous relay. Determine the exact warp around which the lighter butterfly reversed its direction. The next relay of the lighter weft should be two warps to the right of the first. Weave the two butterflies to meet in this position. If the new relay warp is raised in this shed, weave the lighter butterfly under it. However, if the new relay warp is lowered in this shed, wait to carry the lighter butterfly around it in the next shed when it is raised. Logically, the darker weft should relay around the warp directly to the right of the lighter weft. These four rows of weaving have thus produced two complete passes, the second of which resulted in a slight shift of both weft colors toward the right.

Continue weaving in this manner until the first diagonal line is about 3″ (7.5 cm.) long. Remember to increase the lighter area by two warps every other row. Shift the wefts to their new relay position as the butterflies are woven toward each other. The lighter weft can relay around its next warp in either shed. The darker weft will follow logically. The angle will develop precisely if the wefts are shifted with absolute consistency. End the weaving of this example with the butterflies at the selvedges. Observe the low diagonal line with its angle of about 20 degrees.

Next, switch the direction of the diagonal line by gradually increasing the darker area, while concurrently decreasing the lighter area. And at the same time, change the degree of its angle, making it steeper, by increasing the darker area one warp every two rows. In other words, at the next relay, advance the darker color one warp to the left. As before, it is possible to shift the weft colors in either shed. Develop this diagonal line for about 3″. It should have an angle of about 30 degrees.

Once again, switch the direction of the diagonal line and increase the degree of its angle. This time, advance the lighter color one warp to the right, weave four rows (two complete passes) at this relay, then again advance the lighter color one warp to the right. Weaving four rows at each relay position creates a very steep diagonal line between the two weft colors. Develop this example for about 2″. Its angle should measure about 50 degrees.

Finally, switch the direction of the diagonal line and create an angle of about 60 degrees. An angle this steep requires shifting each relay one warp to the left, then weaving six rows in each position. Weave about 2″ of this example.

You have created four diagonal lines between the two weft colors, each with a different degree of angle. Note the steplike effect along the diagonal lines. These steps clearly illustrate the interdependent relationship between warp and weft. Each step represents a shift of position of the two weft colors. The width of a step is the horizontal distance of the color shift. The narrowest step possible would be the distance between two warps (the sett). The height of a step is controlled by the number of rows woven at each position.

Tips & Advice

Firm relays. Weft yarns should be carried firmly around the warps as their direction is reversed along a diagonal line. Otherwise, small loops of weft yarn may appear on the surface of the tapestry, or the diagonal line may develop in an uneven or sloppy manner.

Consistent sheds. To develop the straightest possible line, weft colors should be shifted consistently. A weft color may be shifted to its new relay position in whichever of the two sheds the required warp is raised. But to ensure absolute consistency, do it the same way every time.

Focus on one weft. As a diagonal line develops, one weft color advances while another recedes. It helps a weaver's concentration to focus primarily on only one of the two colors (I usually concentrate on the relays of the advancing weft). The second color then falls into place automatically.

Beating style. Beating style can affect diagonal lines. If the weft is packed very tightly, more rows of weaving may be required to construct a diagonal line, and the degree of its angle may be slightly lowered. Conversely, beating lightly may develop a diagonal line with fewer woven rows and a less acute angle. Obviously, irregular beating would result in a less than perfectly straight diagonal line.

A woven record. Experiment with other degrees of angles on other setts, weaving samples for your own reference with black and white yarns. Measure the angles with a protractor and keep notes as to the sett and the weight of weft yarns used. Because of the many variables in the weaving of diagonal lines, it is useful to have a collection of woven examples to provide a starting point for planning future cartoon interpretations.

Pretest. To achieve a flawless interpretation of a diagonal line from a cartoon, you should weave a small sample of the particular angle. Of course, you can dive in and hope for the best. But, ideally, you should proceed only after you have sampled and determined conclusively the optimum combination of sett, weft yarns, and mathematical progression.

Relating designs to skills. You may also, as you develop preferences for certain successful, diagonal lines, incorporate those particular diagonals into your tapestry designs. By considering only carefully tested and refined tapestry weaving techniques for the interpretation of your cartoons, you will successfully integrate all aspects of design and technique.

Slits. Observe the small slits along the steepest diagonal line, and consider how they might affect the structure of a tapestry. What if there were two or more rows of slits in close proximity? What if a row of slits was positioned near the selvedge in a tapestry to be mounted with the selvedges horizontal? These are very important considerations—even more so in regard to larger, heavier tapestries.

One possible solution would be to interlock the two colors each time they meet. For instance, in the case of the last diagonal line on your sampler, each slit would be replaced by a series of three interlocks. This weft-crossing technique would certainly stabilize the structure of the tapestry, but it would also introduce a sawtooth texture between the two weft colors. Another possibility would be the dovetail technique, which creates a very strong connection but also mingles the two weft colors.

You could, of course, sew each small slit—a time-consuming procedure, but the best solution if it is important to create a clean line between the two weft colors and to stabilize the structure of the tapestry.

Dovetails. A dovetail crossing can also be used along certain diagonal lines for a purely aesthetic purpose. Observe the steps along the first diagonal line—the one created by shifting the weft colors two warps every other row. This particular progression, and any progression involving a shift of weft color over two or more warps, may result in pronounced bumps between the two weft colors. The diagonal line will usually appear perfectly straight on one side of the tapestry, and quite bumpy on the opposite side (use a mirror to check the diagonal line on the reverse side of your tapestry). In some instances, bumps occur along a diagonal line pointing in one direction, then disappear completely as the direction of the line is reversed (as in the weaving of diamond shapes). This can be particularly frustrating if geometric uniformity is important to the design.

The reason for this troublesome inconsistency is simple to understand but sometimes difficult to control. Remember that to construct a diagonal line, one weft color advances while another recedes. A bumpy diagonal line is the result of the advancing weft color relaying around the raised warp as the two colors separate. If the *receding* color relays around the raised warp, the diagonal line is absolutely straight, crisp, and free of bumps.

Navajo Rug, Klagetoh Pattern ("Hidden Springs"). Cotton warp, single-spun wool weft; 31" x 50½" (78 by 126 cm.). Photo: George Mauro. Collection of Carol and Ken Hopper. Stepped diagonals with stepped outlines (outlining geometric shapes).

Bumpy diagonal lines result when the advancing weft color relays around the raised warp as the two colors separate. Straight lines result when the receding color relays around the raised warp.

69

This page and the next: serrated diagonal lines woven on two different setts.

While it is not always possible to plan the exact positions of weft relays along a diagonal line, it is possible to create reasonably straight and, more importantly, consistent diagonal lines by dovetailing the two wefts each time they meet and separate. This weft-crossing technique mashes the two colors together, one on top of the other. While the resulting diagonal line lacks the crisp perfection of those developed by consistently reversing the receding weft around the raised warp, it is easily executed in either shed, around any warp, and according to any progression of color shifts. Because the lower weft color is always carried first around the dovetail warp and because the position of the dovetail is constantly shifting laterally, there is no mingling of the two weft colors and no distortion of texture.

Serrated Diagonal Lines

General Directions

Choose two colors of weft yarn with contrasting hues and values, and make a butterfly with each.

Enter the two butterflies into the next shed at the selvedges, placing the darker color to the left. Weave them to meet at a point about 2″ from the right selvedge. Change sheds and return the butterflies to their respective selvedges. At the first relay, a serrated diagonal line will develop, pointing upward and to the left.

The first example involves a simple six-row repeat. Considering the first relay as rows one and two, weave a total of six rows, shifting the weft colors one warp to the left, every other row. There should be three progressive relays between the two weft colors. The next six-row sequence should begin one warp to the right of the third relay. Interrupting the progression creates a delicate serration. Weave in this manner until the serrated diagonal line is about 2″ long. Observe its subtle, slightly feathered edge.

Next, create a diagonal line with a more dramatic edge. Switch the direction of the diagonal line, pointing the second example upward and to the right. Counting from the last relay of the previous example, weave according to this four-row repeat:

1. Advance the weft colors four warps to the right of the previous relay.
2. Return the butterflies to the selvedges.
3. Back up the next relay to a position two warps to the left of the previous relay.
4. Return the butterflies to the selvedges. (Repeat the sequence.)

Weave this second serrated diagonal line until it is about 2″ long.

Compare the two serrated lines: one delicate and flamelike, the other bold and emphatic. Weave a third of your own design, using any angle or progression you desire. Be creative, even combining two or three progressions in a row before repeating.

Consider the various applications for this technique in a tapestry design. Observe how the handsome and deliberate intermingling of the two colors eliminates any need for controlling slits. Note that the emphatic steps dominating the diagonal lines in the previous section have now become absorbed in the dynamics of the serrations between the two colors.

Tips & Advice

Indian technique. The technique for weaving serrated diagonal lines is similar to one which has been used for generations by the Navajo rug weavers of the American Southwest to create geometric shapes with beautiful feathered edges. And Mexican Indians used "piquete chino," meaning curly edge, to describe complicated zigzag designs on rugs, serapes, and ponchos. Weavers from both of these cultures produced sturdy, completely reversible tapestry-woven textiles with few slits.

Subtle refinements. Serrated diagonal lines are slightly more time-consuming to weave than the usual type, and they require more concentration during the weaving process. But the results are well worth the additional effort.

Complex lines. The pointed edges of the serrations and the intervals between them also form diagonal lines, echoing the stronger angle between the two weft colors.

Counting. When you are planning serrated diagonal lines, it is crucial to establish a precise numerical progression. Counting while weaving should prevent errors.

Pretest. As with other diagonal lines, one color advances while another recedes. How frequently this progression is interrupted, and to what degree, determines the character of the serrated diagonal line. These factors also directly affect the degree of the angle. As with any tapestry technique, to be precise, weave samples.

A Diamond

General Directions

Choose two colors of weft yarn with contrasting hues and values, and make two butterflies with each.

Into the next weaving shed, enter both lighter butterflies, traveling in opposite directions. Relaying the two butterflies at random, weave about ten rows, creating the bottom of the solid-color background into which the diamond shape will be inserted. Rest the two background butterflies at the selvedges.

Determine which warp is the exact center of the row of weaving. With a permanent marker, place a mark on this warp near the reed. The two points at the top and bottom of the diamond shape will be created around this warp. It will also be a point of reference for counting the warps as the weft colors are shifted.

Weave two more rows with the lighter butterflies, reversing their directions around the two warps to either side of the center warp. In other words, leave the center warp unwoven at this time. Then continue weaving with the two lighter butterflies, gradually moving even farther away from the center warp. The relay of the butterfly at the right should be shifted one warp to the right every other row, and the relay of the butterfly at the left should be shifted one warp to the left every other row. Observe the void between the two background areas with its two angled sides.

71

First weave the background for the lower part of the diamond, then the diamond itself, then the background for the upper part.

Expanding both sides of the lower part of the diamond at the same time and by the same amount controls the symmetry of the two converging diagonal lines. Note that the valley of unwoven warps is inaccessible to the loom beater. When this area is eventually woven, a hand beater must be used. Therefore, to maintain a consistent quality throughout the entire example, avoid overpacking the two background areas; beat them with a hand beater as well. Weave in this manner until each of the two background areas measures about 2″ from the selvedge.

Next, determine the correct shed for weaving the first row of the diamond. This is important, because the rows of the diamond shape should correspond to the rows of the background in exactly the same manner as they would if the two weft colors were meeting and separating at the same time. Carefully observe the two warps indicating the first shift of background color away from the center warp. Should the next row of weaving travel under or over these two warps? The answer to this question will determine the correct shed for weaving the first narrow (three-warp) row of the diamond.

First, open the correct shed for weaving the first row of the diamond, then wrap the tails of the two darker butterflies from both directions around the center warp. These weft tails should protrude from the back of the tapestry from opposite sides of the center warp, and will be tied to one another during the finishing process. This wrapping procedure, if it is executed correctly, enters both darker butterflies into the tiny space at the bottom of the diamond, traveling in opposite directions. Check that the butterflies are positioned to travel correctly over the row of weaving in which the background color was first shifted. Observe that wrapping the tails of both butterflies around the center warp introduced a double amount of the darker weft yarn around that warp. As this loaded warp is beaten, the yarn should be forced slightly into the last row of background forming the bottom point of the diamond.

With the two darker butterflies, weave one complete pass (two very short rows). Observe that the darker weft has shifted one warp away from the center warp as a result of the weaving of these two rows. Beating with a hand beater, proceed with the weaving of the entire bottom of the diamond, until the darker area is level with the lighter area. Increase the width woven by the darker wefts to correspond exactly with the shifts of the lighter wefts. As the bottom of the diamond increases in width, maneuvering the two butterflies becomes easier.

When the diamond is level with the background, continue weaving with the two darker butterflies. Develop the top of the diamond by shifting the darker wefts two warps closer to the center warp every other row. This will create symmetrical diagonal lines of a different degree from those along the bottom of the diamond. To prevent overbeating, beat the top of the diamond with a hand beater.

When only one warp remains at the top of the diamond, wrap each of the dark butterflies around it and tuck their tails to the back of the tapestry. The diamond is complete.

Weave the two remaining background areas, one side at a time, beating with the hand beater. When the woven area again becomes level, weave the two lighter butterflies toward each other, meeting at any point across the row. Relaying the two butterflies at random, weave about ten more rows of background, building a solid-color area the same width as the base below the diamond.

Tips & Advice

Slit control. The tiny slit at the bottom of the diamond results from the two darker butterflies relaying in a very narrow space. This is not a problem. The diamond shape quickly expands to include a greater number of warps, providing more relay positions for the two butterflies. To avoid a slit altogether, dovetail the two butterflies around the center warp once or twice.

Consistency. Symmetrical diagonal lines, whether they describe positive contours (the diamond) or negative ones (the background), are easily created with absolute precision if they are developed row by row with two butterflies traveling in opposite directions. One reason is that weft colors can be easily shifted to any position, every other row. Another reason is that the actions of both butterflies are mirror images. In other words, both relays occur around raised warps in one shed and lowered warps in the other. Thus if a converging pair of diagonal lines has been woven with butterflies traveling in opposite directions, the corresponding rows along these lines must be woven in the same manner.

For example, if the bottom of the diamond shape had been filled in with a single butterfly (an attractive option, considering the narrow space at the point of the diamond), the rows woven with that single butterfly would have corresponded correctly to the rows of the background at only one side of the diamond. Because the background was woven with two butterflies traveling in opposite directions, two opposing butterflies are required for weaving the diamond.

Conversely, the background areas at both sides of the top of the diamond can only be woven with two separate butterflies. Therefore, to ensure again that the rows of the background and the rows of the diamond correspond exactly, the top of the diamond must also be woven with two butterflies.

Many weavers insert geometric shapes into a background by weaving with butterflies all traveling in the same direction. This technique is quite acceptable and certainly makes inserting or deleting butterflies less complicated. But weft colors cannot be shifted around quite as neatly or expediently with this method.

What to weave first. Think about the order in which you wove the diamond and the sides of the background. Two sets of diagonal lines were developed. The first set defined the sides of the bottom of the background, and the second set defined the top of the diamond. In both cases, the areas within the lines inclined in an upward direction, underneath another area. Logically, these underneath areas must always be woven first.

Entering a new color. Remember to begin weaving in the correct shed and in the correct direction as you introduce another weft color along a previously woven diagonal line. The two weft colors must line up as precisely as if they were woven at the same time. Check that every warp is covered and that there are no floats over two or more warps.

Applications. This particular example provides important experience with developing valuable tapestry skills not necessarily related to the weaving of diamond shapes. For instance, the example is not woven row by row. By focusing on the creation of an individual shape, you develop judgment, confidence, and greater control over the precise placement of weft colors. When you weave certain sections separately, it becomes quite apparent that woven warps adjacent to unwoven warps may be vulnerable to distortions, requiring even more meticulous handling of the weft. In

In reality one works with few colors. What gives the illusion of their being many is simply the fact that they have been put in the right place.

—Pablo Picasso

addition, the importance of assigning the correct weaving sequence to each section is demonstrated by the development of these simple shapes. And, when you examine a diagonal line with its edge exposed, the weft relays and the sheds in which they were made can be seen clearly, directing the correct moves for filling in along the line.

Other considerations. When designing triangles or diamonds for a tapestry, consider all the technical tricks from the previous sections on diagonal lines. Consider scale, degree of angle, and quality of line. These shapes can be very effective if defined by serrated diagonal lines or exaggerated steps.

Horizontal and vertical symmetry. Because the diagonal lines at the top of the diamond were constructed with a different angle from those at the bottom, this particular diamond is horizontally symmetrical, but not vertically symmetrical. Horizontal symmetry is achieved by consistently shifting the weft colors the same amount in both directions at the same time. Vertical symmetry is achieved by weaving accurate mirror images of the angles of the lower diagonal lines. Beating may also have an effect on vertical symmetry.

Vertical Curves

General Directions

Choose two colors of weft yarn with contrasting hues and values, and make a butterfly with each.

Trace the curved line from the cartoon on page 169 onto heavy tracing paper. Pin or clip the tracing paper to the warps, placing the bottom line on the last row of weaving. The X should be positioned about 2″ from the left selvedge. With a permanent marker, mark each intersection of line and warp by placing small dots directly onto the warps. Remove the paper. Extend the dots to completely circle the warps: Hold the point of the marker on the original dot with one hand and spin the warp between your thumb and index finger with your other hand. (Adjusting the tension or advancing the weaving space may cause the warps to rotate.)

Enter the two butterflies into the next weaving shed at the selvedges, placing the lighter color to the right. Weave them toward each other to meet at the first dotted warp. Reverse the direction of the lighter butterfly around the dotted warp. Continue weaving row by row, meeting and separating the butterflies, placing the two weft colors along the dotted curved line. As each mark disappears under the weft, shift the butterflies to the next position, always placing the lighter color to cover the dots. Weave until the curved line is complete. Rest the two butterflies at the selvedges.

In the same manner as before, pin or clip the cartoon to the warps and again trace the curved line. This time, as you develop the line, dovetail the butterflies around the dotted warps. Execute the dovetail either as the butterflies meet or as they separate, but consistently place the receding color below the other around the common warp. As the curved line becomes steeper, requiring several dovetails in succession around the same warp, the characteristic sawtooth effect will occur. Using the dovetail technique along a curved line constructs a completely secure connection between the two colors of yarn, an important consideration for very large or heavy tapestries mounted with the warps horizontal.

It is all this one kind of weave, just back and forth, very simple, like sketching but side to side. Like bricklaying in a way.

—Julia Mitchell

Next, draw a vertical curved line of your own design. With the same two weft colors, interpret it using any or all of the following techniques: meeting and separating, dovetail, single weft interlock. Compare the woven effects and the quality of the line. More than any other cartoon interpretation, vertical curved lines require visual judgment, a result of experimentation, experience, and observation.

Tips & Advice

Placing relays. The first experiment, using the meeting and separating technique, requires placing one of the two weft colors along the dotted warps. In the example, either weft color could cover the dots without significantly affecting the design; but as you begin to interpret actual tapestry cartoons, this decision becomes more crucial. On a tapestry cartoon, a line appears to travel between two colors. However, weaving along a dotted line on the warps creates a specific contour, defining a shape within the tapestry design. Consider this shape and its relationship to the background when assigning a color to cover the dots. By doing so, you accurately define volumes, sizes, and proportions.

A dovetailed line. In the dovetail experiment, both weft colors are carried around the marked warps, every other row. This creates a line in the tapestry in the same position as the line on the cartoon.

Single and double interlocks. Other techniques to consider for weaving vertical curved lines are the single weft interlock and the double weft interlock. Either of these techniques can be introduced as needed to prevent slits, but you may prefer the visual consistency of using the single weft interlock all along a vertical curve. Remember that the double weft interlock must be woven from the reverse side of the tapestry.

Raised vs. lowered warps. As with the technique for developing diagonal lines, the interpretation of vertical curved lines requires one weft color to advance while another recedes. Some of the same circumstances occur with both techniques. For instance, if a curved line is being developed with the meeting and separating technique, shifting the weft colors one warp every other row creates a very smooth line. However, shifting the weft colors two or more warps every other row can create seemingly inexplicable bumps along the line. These occur only if the advancing weft color reverses its direction around the raised warp between the two wefts. If you are weaving a design with jagged, free-form lines, the tiny bumps will not be intrusive, and in some instances they may be desirable. But if your design demands only smooth curved lines, be sure to reverse the direction of the receding weft color around the raised warp between the two wefts. Of course, if the tapestry is being woven from the reverse side, the opposite rule would apply.

Artistic judgment. Dots on the warps are intended only to direct the approximate placement of adjacent weft colors; your eyes and experience should guide every decision. As you weave, watch the line grow, check the cartoon frequently, and make adjustments based on your assessment of how the line should appear in the tapestry. Rigid adherence to a dotted line may produce a paint-by-numbers effect.

Personal style. Study the tapestries used to illustrate this technique. Observe the lines as they travel upward, jumping from warp to warp. Look for evidence of dovetail or interlocking techniques as the line becomes very steep. Think about the quality of lines as they relate to specific tapestries.

The custom of burying the dead in their own garments has left a rich legacy of Coptic textiles. Highly skilled Egyptian weavers worked a garment all in one piece on the loom, including the sleeves. The plain linen fabric of garments was worked with colored wool wefts to produce decorative panels of woven tapestry. Often only these patterned portions survived.

—Dr. Susan Auth, Curator of Antiquities, The Newark Museum

Lines that appear to be flowing and smooth are usually woven with consistency of technique on a very fine sett. Jagged, uneven lines use the warp/weft grid to create these dynamic characteristics. The lines that a weaver/designer uses to create a design and the manner in which these lines are interpreted in the tapestry are important elements in the development of personal style. You will certainly discover your own preferences and prejudices for certain types of lines. Exploit these lines to their fullest potential, and watch your distinctive style emerge.

Criteria. When deciding how to join colors along a vertical curved line, consider the woven effects of each of the techniques, your personal style and preferences, the size and weight of the tapestry, and the direction from which it will be mounted.

Fourth-century Coptic medallion with a head of Dionysius. Tapestry over paired and triple warps, slit and dovetailed; eccentric wefts. Warp of undyed linen, weft of undyed linen, purple and tan wool. Collection of the Textile Museum, Washington, D.C.

A Doughnut

General Directions

Choose a weft yarn with a very light value for weaving the background around the doughnut and the circle inside; make four butterflies. Next, choose a weft yarn for the doughnut, contrasting in value and hue with the first color; make two butterflies.

Enter two of the lighter butterflies into the next weaving shed traveling in opposite directions. Relaying the two butterflies at random, weave about 1″ (2.5 cm.) of background. Rest the two butterflies at the selvedges.

Trace the doughnut shape and its horizontal and vertical reference lines from page 169 onto heavy tracing paper. Pin or clip the paper to the warps, placing the doughnut directly above the last row of weaving. The vertical line should be placed along the center warp. The line itself need not be traced, but the center warp should be marked near the reed and re-marked as the weaving proceeds. The horizontal line will provide valuable reference points at the halfway mark; it should be traced. Trace the doughnut shape and the horizontal line onto the warps by placing a dot at every intersection of line and warp. In the same manner as in the previous section, extend the dots to circle the warps.

Continue weaving with the two lighter butterflies, creating the background areas surrounding the bottom half of the doughnut. As always, when packing incomplete rows, beat with a hand beater. Shift the two butterflies symmetrically, following the dots on the warps. When the background has been woven to the horizontal line, rest the two butterflies at the selvedges.

Open the correct shed for weaving the next row at the bottom of the doughnut, and enter the two darker butterflies, traveling in opposite directions, toward the selvedges. Their tails should be overlapped over the center warp, and their first complete pass (two very short rows) should include the two warps adjacent to the center warp. By entering the darker yarn over a broad three-warp area, you avoid creating a point at the bottom of the doughnut. When developing any woven round shape, square off its sides, top, and bottom slightly. Even though it seems logical to build a circle outward at these four crucial positions, to do so creates small interruptions along the curve. Because these interruptions involve only one or two warps, they look like points and appear unrelated to the carefully executed roundness of the rest of the circle.

76

Continue weaving with the two darker butterflies, meeting the background symmetrically row by row from both directions. Until the darker weft color reaches the dots marking the inside ring of the doughnut, the two butterflies should relay at random. Then they should travel upward separately, to weave the sides of the doughnut. Follow the rows of the background in one shed and the dots marking the inside of the doughnut in the opposite shed. When the sides of the doughnut are level with the background, rest the two darker butterflies at the sides.

Enter the remaining two lighter butterflies at the bottom of the doughnut hole in the same manner as the two darker butterflies were entered. Weave until the doughnut hole is complete. As you weave the top half of the circle, concentrate on creating a mirror image of the lower half, using as a guide the most valuable weaver's reference—an existing woven shape and diameter. If necessary, deviate from the dotted line. To check its symmetry, measure the diameter of the circle from side to side, top to bottom, and diagonally. End the two lighter butterflies over three warps, overlapping their tails around the center warp.

Next, weave the remaining half of the doughnut. Keep the width of the doughnut consistent, building curves across the top that are mirror images of the curves across the bottom. End the two darker butterflies.

Complete the weaving of the background around both sides and over the top of the doughnut. End the last two lighter butterflies.

Tips & Advice

Warp tension. Tracing a precise geometric shape from a cartoon should be done onto a warp that is taut but not stretched tight. Then, as the tension is tightened for weaving, the dotted lines become slightly elongated vertically. Weave according to these minor distortions, but realize that as the tapestry is removed from the tension of the loom, the design will relax to its intended proportions. It is, however, quite important to weave with a consistent degree of tension, not only to ensure the correct measurements, but to establish a uniform woven quality throughout the tapestry. Train your hands to test the tension of the warps each time you advance the weaving space, always adjusting to the same degree of tension.

Symmetry. How does a weaver control symmetry in a geometric tapestry design? Perfect horizontal symmetry is created by the moves of the weft colors—by symmetrically shifting the positions of opposing, adjacent weft colors. This is true for negative shapes (the background) and positive ones (the doughnut and the diamond).

Vertical symmetry requires creating a mirror image over a previously woven shape. The upper half should contain the same number of rows as the lower half, and the wefts of both halves must be beaten with equal force. Keeping the tension of the warps and the slight vertical distortion consistent also helps. Measuring frequently can be very reassuring.

Diagonal symmetry should happen naturally. If the upper and lower halves of a shape are mirror images and the right and left halves mirror each other, then the opposite quadrants will also be perfect.

Crowded butterflies. Maneuvering two butterflies of the same color across a very narrow space, such as the bottom of a circle, requires special attention. Slits or small holes may occur, as a result of relaying two wefts in close quarters. To conveniently heal these tiny slits, dovetail both wefts around a common warp. If you turn the wefts firmly around the warp and

Jan Yoors, Vermillion Tantra. Woven by Annabert Yoors. Cotton warp, wool weft; 8′ x 10′ (2.4 by 3 m.); 1976. Photo: Marianne Yoors.

carefully shift around the position of the dovetails, the crossing technique is quite invisible. As the shape grows wider, you can again employ the meeting and separating technique, or do as I do—dovetail randomly all small, solid-color areas woven with two opposing butterflies.

Sett. Compare the smooth, round curves along the tops and bottoms of the circles with the prominent steps along the steep curves at the sides. The contours vary because the curves at the top and bottom are developed by shifting the weft color over one or two warps at a time, creating a fluid line; the curves at the sides are developed by relaying adjacent weft colors several rows in succession around the same warp—the result being emphatic steps. If smooth, graceful curves are important to your tapestry interpretations, take the sett into consideration when planning a design. A closer sett provides more positions for shifting weft colors, resulting in more fluid curves. A wider sett provides fewer positions, resulting in distinct steps along a vertical curve.

Regine Bartsch, Relativity. *Linen warp, wool weft; 48″ x 48″ (120 by 120 cm.); 1983.*

Constance Hunt, Sisters: A Family Portrait. Cotton warp, wool weft; 48″ x 64″ (120 by 160 cm.); 1987. Photo: Gary Hunt.

Laura Shannock, Divergence. Cotton warp, wool weft; 59″ x 45″ (148 by 113 cm.); 1986. Photo: John Shannock. Collection of Robert I. Kligman. Double weft interlock, hachures, color blending on the bobbin.

VERTICAL LINES

Joyce Hulbert, And So the Story Goes . . .
Cotton warp, hand-dyed wool weft; 30″ x 21″
(75 by 53 cm.); 1986. Hachures, double weft
interlock.

Jan Yoors, Fishermen. Woven by Annabert
and Marianne Yoors. Cotton warp, wool weft;
6′ x 15′ (1.8 by 4.5 m.). Photo by George
Cserna.

VERTICAL LINES

Care Standley, Stripes. Wool, cotton materials; 21″ x 41″ (53 by 103 cm.); 1985. Photo: Kim Carson. Collection of Vincent Crisci.

Susan Guagliumi, El color es la canción Mexicana y todo el pueblo canta. Linen warp, wool Swedish singles weft; 51″ x 68″ (128 by 170 cm.); 1983. Photo: Arthur Guagliumi. Collection of Lawry's Foods, Los Angeles, California.

Margaretta Grandin Nettles, Flower Bed.
Linen warp; wool, linen, and silk weft; 9½″ x
10½″ (24 by 26 cm.). Photo: Jack Weinhold.

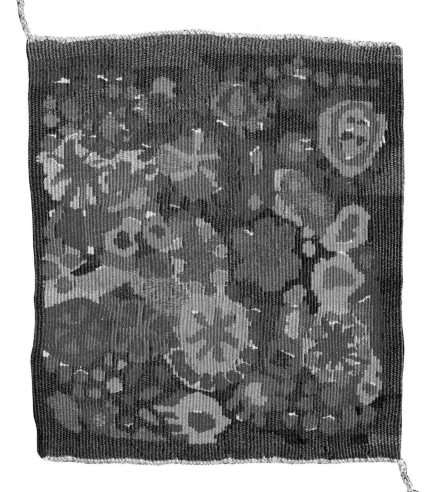

Mona Elise Rummel, Lepidoptera (detail).
Cotton warp; wool, mohair, silk, and rayon
weft; 37″ x 42″ (93 by 105 cm.); 1980.
Reversible tapestry technique.

Christine Lafer, Rhythm and Blues. Wool warp and weft; 60″ x 96″ (150 by 240 cm.); 1988-89. Photo: Jacques Cressaty. Collection of F. R. and P. L. Holt.

Sharon Marcus, Time Marker. Cotton, wool, and goat hair materials; 59½″ x 38″ (149 by 95 cm.); 1989. Photo: Bill Bachhuber.

VERTICAL LINES

Care Standley, Cypress Swamp. Cotton warp, wool weft; 20″ x 30″ (50 by 75 cm.); 1984. Photo: Peter Macchia.

Elaine Ireland, Melody. Woven by Susan Hart Henegar Studio. Cotton warp, wool weft; 48″ x 73″ (120 by 183 cm.); 1980. Photo: Don Beatty. Collection of The Fairmont Hotel, San Francisco, California.

Shading Techniques

5

This chapter explains several tapestry techniques for creating woven gradations. As it pertains to the shading of forms in two-dimensional art, a gradation is a gradual transition from one hue, value, or intensity to another. By subtly blending pigments, a painter can portray roundness of form, depth of space, or source of light. Tapestry weavers attempting those same descriptions have an additional challenge: constructing the body of the tapestry while interpreting its images. Although more illusory than a painter's, a weaver's gradations communicate hearty shadings from deep within the woven texture, imparting a special richness as well as a precision unique to the art of tapestry.

To portray a rounded form within a tapestry, you must weave carefully graded intervals of value, shifting from darker to lighter and back again. Or a sunset may be designed with shaded streaks of purple and orange. The success of such designs cannot be the result of haphazard yarn splashing. Appropriate hue and value choices, combined with control of technique, will elevate a tapestry from a merely amateurish to a professional level.

Most tapestry weavers, as they gain experience with the craft, limit their repertoire of shading devices to a preferred few. Each of the techniques explained in this chapter produces different color interactions and textural effects. To further complicate the selection process, certain shading techniques can be successfully applied in only one direction—horizontal or vertical. By experimenting with shading techniques from various weaving traditions, and by creating examples of their impact on color relationships, you will have a beautiful record of woven possibilities. But more than that, as your personal style emerges, you will have an informed basis for selecting those techniques that most appropriately interpret and communicate your tapestry designs.

Gradations of Dots

General Directions

From your supply of weft yarns, choose two values of the same hue. For instance, you may have a dark and a light violet, or two contrasting values of the same blue-green, or white and medium gray. The darker yarn will be used for the background of this example and the lighter yarn for the dots. Make a butterfly with each of these weft yarns.

Enter the darker butterfly at either selvedge and weave about ½″ (1.25 cm.) of background. Observe the actions of the selvedge warps as you weave this solid-color area. In one shed the selvedge warps are lowered, and in the opposite shed they are raised. The lighter butterfly should be entered into the shed with raised selvedge warps. Therefore, rest the background butterfly after it has been woven through the shed with lowered selvedge warps. The lighter butterfly can then be entered in either direction. The gradation will be created by interspersing rows of dots between graded intervals of background. Since the lighter butterfly will not be carried around the selvedge warps, the dots will be neatly contained within the selvedges. After each row of dots has been woven, drop the lighter butterfly to the reverse side of the tapestry. From this position it can invisibly reenter the tapestry as needed. Carry the darker butterfly twice around the selvedge warp at the beginning of each background interval to compensate for its having been skipped by the lighter butterfly in the previous row.

Using the following progression, weave the first gradation. This precisely planned distribution of dots will appear to shade the woven example from a lighter to a relatively darker value. To "shade" a color means to lower, or darken, its relative value.

1. One pick of dots, three picks of background. (Repeat these four rows, three times.)
2. One pick of dots, five picks of background. (Repeat these six rows, three times.)
3. One pick of dots, seven picks of background. (Repeat these eight rows, three times.)

As greater intervals of darker-value background appear between the rows of lighter-value dots, observe that the example appears to become progressively darker—in other words, shaded. Also, note that the dots are organized into rigid horizontal and vertical rows.

Using the following formula, weave the second gradation. This example will use the same shading device, although the progression of the gradation will be reversed and the dots will not be organized vertically. As before, avoid carrying the lighter butterfly around the selvedge warps. Compensate the skipped selvedge warps with extra wraps of background weft, steering any unavoidable floats to the reverse side of the tapestry.

1. One pick of dots, six picks of background. (Repeat these seven rows, three times.)
2. One pick of dots, four picks of background. (Repeat these five rows, three times.)
3. One pick of dots, two picks of background. (Repeat these three rows, three times.)

Notice that placing rows of dots in both sheds has created a random, scattered effect. The rigid horizontal and vertical organization of the previous example has been relaxed, while the progression between values has reversed. In this case the value of the example appears to have been gradually lightened—in other words, tinted. To "tint" a color means to raise, or lighten, its relative value.

Next, experiment with placing dots throughout the weave in a freeform manner. Open the next weaving shed; introduce the lighter butterfly into the shed from the reverse side of the tapestry; carry it through the shed from any point and across any distance. In the same shed, weave background color from selvedge to selvedge, floating the darker butterfly behind the area of dots. Observe the woven row. Every lowered warp should be covered, but none should be covered twice. The lighter yarn may emerge from the reverse side of the tapestry, designating an isolated area of dots. The darker yarn should be woven from selvedge to selvedge, dropping temporarily to the back of the tapestry to float behind the dotted area. With the expertise you've acquired in weaving the two previous examples, design spontaneously, placing the dots in any position and at any intervals you choose. End the lighter butterfly at the completion of the dotted experiment. Weave about ½″ of background to finish the example.

Tips & Advice

Selvedges. To keep the selvedges uncluttered, restrict the dots to the warps inside the selvedges. After you have woven a row of dots, drop the butterfly below the work, missing one or two warps at the selvedge. This creates a small vertical loop on the reverse side of the tapestry as the

Introducing scattered dots by carrying a background weft across the row, floating it below any warps covered by the "dot" weft.

contrasting weft reenters the shed for weaving the next row of dots. The loops are invisible from the front of the tapestry, and they are structurally sound. This is also a clever trick to use when reintroducing a color a few rows above its last appearance.

Placing dots. Weaving an uneven number of background rows between rows of dots keeps the dots consistently in the same shed. Thus, the dots will line up vertically. Weaving an even number of background rows between rows of dots shifts the dots back and forth between two horizontal positions. Therefore, the dots appear more random in their placement, and a strong vertical element has been eliminated.

Never weave only one row of background weft between two rows of dots. To do so stacks the contrasting rows directly above one another, creating the narrow vertical stripes of the pick-and-pick technique.

Subtle contrasts. As a shading device, dots are most successful when they are closely related to the background in value, hue, and intensity. When viewed from a distance, dots blend with the background, appearing as a subtle shift of value.

Butterflies. In the spontaneous experiment, the background butterfly will be woven every row, traveling from selvedge to selvedge and floating behind any dotted segments. The contrasting butterfly will be woven only across designated areas of certain rows. This butterfly can be introduced into the shed from the back of the tapestry at any point, woven through the shed from either direction, and returned to the back of the tapestry at any point.

Weaving from front or back. As you weave this narrow sampler, it is possible to reach both butterflies at all times, whether they are resting conveniently at the selvedges or behind the work. On a wider tapestry, a weaver cannot comfortably reach behind the work, making it difficult to carry a contrasting butterfly on the reverse side. As you begin to weave larger, more personal tapestries, you will realize that tapestry techniques are frequently chosen according to a weaver's preferred method of working. If a tapestry is very wide and you wish to sprinkle colors around at will, you must plan to weave it from the reverse side. Conversely, if you prefer weaving your tapestries from the right side, you must employ only those techniques that can be executed from the front.

Isolated dots. It is possible to interject an isolated row of dots into the weave. Lay a length of contrasting weft over the lowered warps, covering the desired distance. Drop the tails, which should be at least 3″ (7.5 cm.) long, to the back of the tapestry. In the same shed, weave the background butterfly across the row as usual, floating it below the dotted area. Even a single dot may be woven in this manner.

Applications. The creative applications of this technique are numerous. Areas of dots woven with highly contrasting yarns can be applied as textures or patterns. Dots can be interjected along the edge of a shape, softening and shading its contours. Even a single, strategically placed dot can have significance in a design. Remember that hue and value relationships between dots and their surrounding areas can either emphasize or moderate the result.

Scattering dots over a woven area is sometimes referred to as "seeding." The textural or shaded effect is much the same as that of the embroidery technique of the same name. But unlike embroidery stitches, woven dots are not merely applied to a previously prepared surface. Their position in the tapestry, and their color relationships, must be carefully planned.

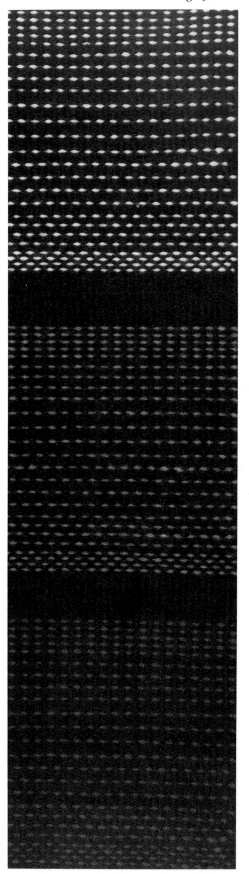

Gradations of dots in three value relationships: strong contrast (black and white), moderate contrast (black and medium gray), and little contrast (black and dark gray).

Fifty-Fifty Wavy Stripes

General Directions

Choose two colors of weft yarn with highly contrasting values, and make a butterfly with each. Enter the darker butterfly at either selvedge and weave two rows. Enter the lighter yarn at the same selvedge and weave two rows. Continue weaving in this manner, alternating two consecutive rows with each butterfly. Weave at least 1½″ (3.75 cm.) of this example. Observe the fine, wavy lines.

End the darker butterfly after a two-pick sequence, leaving the lighter butterfly resting at the selvedge. Choose another weft yarn, one more closely related in hue and value to the lighter butterfly. For instance, if the lighter butterfly is mint green, the new weft could be celadon. Or if the resting butterfly is peach, the new weft could be light pink. Make a butterfly with the new weft yarn.

At the reed measure approximately 1″ (2.5 cm.) from the left selvedge, and mark the nearest warp with a permanent marker. Repeat the procedure at the right selvedge. Enter the new butterfly at the selvedge opposite the resting butterfly, and weave it to the farthest marked warp. If the marked warp is lowered, carry the butterfly out of the shed between the raised warps to either side. If the marked warp is raised, carry the butterfly out of the shed to one side of it. Weave the resting butterfly to meet the new one. Change sheds, reverse the directions of both butterflies, and return them to their respective selvedges. Either butterfly can be carried around the marked warps, but do so consistently throughout this example. Change sheds, and weave the original butterfly to the marked warp nearest the opposite selvedge. Weave the new butterfly to meet it. Change sheds, reverse the directions of both butterflies, and return them to the selvedges. You have thus created, in the center area, two wavy rows of the original color over two wavy rows of the new color.

Continue to construct the example in the following manner:
1. Weave the butterflies to meet at the marked warp opposite the previous relay. (Change sheds.)
2. Weave the butterflies back to the selvedges. (Change sheds.)
3. Weave the butterflies to meet at the opposite marked warp. (Change sheds.)
4. Weave the butterflies back to the selvedges. (Change sheds.)

While the relays of the wefts should alternate between the two marked warps, the butterflies always return to the same selvedges, building areas of solid color to both sides of the striped area in the center. Weave at least 2″ (5 cm.) of this example. End both butterflies at the selvedges.

Tips & Advice

Two-pick lines. Two-pick stripes in contrasting colors are distinctly wavy, an effect created by weaving the two picks into opposite sheds. The first pick delineates the bottom of the line covering alternate warps. The second pick delineates the top of the line covering the opposite alternate warps. The two-pick line is, in effect, two dotted lines offset and closely packed.

Applications. An interesting application of two-pick horizontal lines would be to create a visual effect similar in scale and emphasis to that of the narrow vertical lines created by the pick-and-pick technique. The two

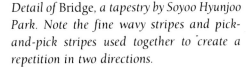

Detail of Bridge, *a tapestry by Soyoo Hyunjoo Park. Note the fine wavy stripes and pick-and-pick stripes used together to create a repetition in two directions.*

techniques can be cleverly combined in a tapestry design, expressing a repetition of harmonic patterns from opposite directions.

Weft-face rugs. As demonstrated in your example, the impressive pattern of two-pick wavy stripes traveling from selvedge to selvedge would be quite effective in a weft-face rug, because the selvedges can be constructed in a neat, reversible manner. One selvedge takes care of itself because the two butterflies never arrive there at the same time. At the other selvedge, carry the butterfly that is being woven around the yarn of the butterfly that must wait for two rows. By carrying both colors around the selvedge warp, you retain the continuity of the narrow stripes across the woven surface and around both selvedges.

Optical blends. With closely related hues and values, the weft colors interact and blend visually in the intermediate striped area. While the technique results in a certain degree of horizontal texture, the wavy edges of the lines actually enhance the potential for creating a successful optical blend. Experiment further with other combinations of hues and values, each of which illustrates a different texture, character, and blending possibility. Observe that the distance and angle from which these combinations are viewed may influence the ultimate effect.

Fifty-fifty wavy stripes used to create a transparent effect.

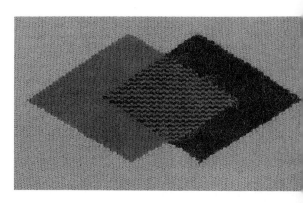

With this technique, you can create the illusion of a transparent color. An area of fine, optically blended stripes between solid areas of two related colors can produce an illusion of transparency between the colors. A rainy afternoon would be well spent experimenting with weaving an assortment of color transparencies, combining as many closely related pairs as possible. By weaving these small samples, you build your weaving skills and create a valuable record of specific color interactions.

Gradations of Lines

General Directions

Choose two weft yarns of the same hue but with a moderate degree of value contrast. For instance, both colors may be green, but one should be slightly darker than the other. Make a butterfly with each of these weft yarns.

With a permanent marker, mark two warps near the reed. One warp should be about 2″ from the left selvedge, the other about 2″ from the right one.

At either selvedge, enter the darker of the two butterflies. With this butterfly traveling from selvedge to selvedge, weave about ½″ of solid color. Rest the darker butterfly at the right selvedge. Into the next shed, enter the lighter butterfly at the left selvedge. Weave it to the marked warp nearest the right selvedge; then weave the darker butterfly to meet the lighter one. Change sheds and return the two butterflies to their respective selvedges.

You have just created the first light line of this gradation. Proceeding in a similar manner to the wavy lines, construct a stack of horizontal lines between the two marked warps. The darker lines should appear narrow and wavy, as each one is created with two picks. The lighter lines gradually expand in width (rows of weaving) to force the narrow, darker lines progressively farther apart—thereby shifting the dominance of value. Both butterflies should participate in the weaving of every row. If a butterfly is involved in creating a line, it should travel to the marked warp nearest the opposite selvedge. If a butterfly is covering only its background, it should

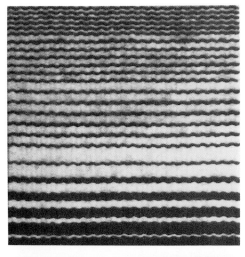

The two types of gradations of lines: (1) keeping the width of the dark weft consistent and (2) grading both values. Woven in three degrees of value contrasts, the gradations create very different effects.

travel to the nearest marked warp. Always return each butterfly to its respective selvedge.

The following progression is an example of tinting—that is, the dominance of value shifts from dark to light.

1. Two picks of lighter weft, two picks of darker weft. (Repeat these four rows, four times.)
2. Four picks of lighter weft, two picks of darker weft. (Repeat these six rows, four times.)
3. Six picks of lighter weft, two picks of darker weft. (Repeat these eight rows, four times.) Rest both butterflies at the selvedges.

This next example becomes gradually darker. Also, the method for organizing a gradation of lines changes. Again, create alternating lines in the area between the marked warps. This time, however, gradually increase the width (rows of weaving) of the darker lines while decreasing the width of the lighter lines. This adjustment of proportions should appear to shade the example, shifting the dominance of value from light to dark. Use the following 13-step formula to develop this gradation:

1. Twelve picks of light.	8. Eight picks of dark.
2. Two picks of dark.	9. Four picks of light.
3. Ten picks of light.	10. Ten picks of dark.
4. Four picks of dark.	11. Two picks of light.
5. Eight picks of light.	12. Twelve picks of dark.
6. Six picks of dark.	13. Two picks of light.
7. Six picks of light.	

Step 13 separates the gradation from the solid-color border. After this step, end the lighter butterfly. Then weave about ½″ of solid color with the darker butterfly, balancing the dark border at the beginning of the first gradation of lines.

Tips & Advice

Straight sides. As you weave the two gradations, maintain straight edges along the sides of the shaded area. Mark the warps as often as necessary, or simply train your eye to reverse the wefts around the same warps every time. Developing these valuable skills improves a weaver's on-the-spot judgment, thereby accelerating the weaving process.

Size of gradations. To create a sizable example of the first gradation, you wove four repeats of each lighter interval. The number of rows required to develop the gradation could be reduced by repeating each interval only once or twice. Or you could elongate the gradation by repeating each interval more times.

Applications. A tapestry may be designed with a very small area in which to develop a gradation. In this case, because a gradation of lines cannot be fully developed on a small scale, it may not be the appropriate choice of shading technique. In a geometric or large-scale design, gradations of lines can be quite successful.

Width of lines. The lines are always created with an even number of picks. (Conversely, lines can be reduced in width only by even numbers of picks.) Remember, the butterflies were returned to the selvedges every other row. Therefore, to make a line wider and to keep the butterflies coordinated, two picks must be added to the previous width. Theoretically, lines of any width can be created, but an excessively wide, dominant line may obscure the relationships within the gradation. It is an excellent idea to view samples of gradations from a distance, tacked to a vertical surface. Under these circumstances, you can judge how successful the visual effect is or how far the technique can be exploited.

Exaggerated stripes. A striped gradation on an exaggerated scale is less a shading device than an emphatic geometric progression. Don't overlook this clever application for tapestry or rug design.

Lines of more than two picks. Observe that woven lines lose their characteristic wavy effect if they are created with more than two picks. While wavy edges in very close proximity emphasize each other, the emphasis is lost as a narrow, wavy line expands, describing instead a bold stripe.

Counting rows. The blunt point of a weaving needle makes a useful tool for counting woven rows. Both of the examples in this section require the weaving of precise numbers of rows to ensure the success of the gradations.

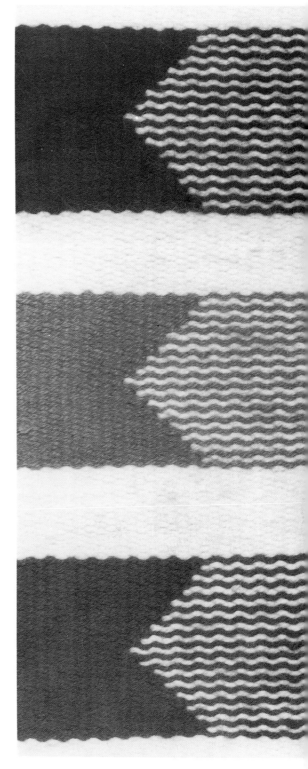

Basic Hatching Technique

General Directions

Two of the previous sections introduced methods for constructing carefully graded intervals of contrasting weft colors, shading vertically between the colors. Another section introduced a method for approximating a half-tone between adjacent weft colors in a communal zone of fine wavy lines. The technique of basic hatching, a further evolution of these methods, is a tool for blending adjacent weft colors horizontally along a mutual vertical contour. To "hatch" is the correct verb form; "hatching" or "hachure" are both commonly used nouns.

To accentuate the woven effects of the hatchings, choose two colors of weft yarn with a high degree of value and/or hue contrast. Make a butterfly with each.

Into the next shed, enter the lighter butterfly at either selvedge, and weave about ½″ of solid color. Rest the lighter butterfly at the left selvedge. Enter the darker butterfly at the right selvedge, and weave it to a point about 2″ from the left selvedge. Weave the lighter butterfly to the same point. Change sheds and return the butterflies to their respective selvedges.

Next, weave the butterflies to meet at a point about 4″ (10 cm.) from the right selvedge. Change sheds and return the butterflies to their respective selvedges. At the left relay, reverse the directions of the butterflies around the same two warps—in other words, repeat rows one and two. At the right relay, however, reverse the directions of the butterflies one warp to the right of the previous relay. Therefore, to weave rows seven and eight, shift the position of the relay one warp to the right, then return the butterflies to their respective selvedges.

Four picks are required to advance each lighter hatching one step to the right—two picks for weaving to the left relay and back to the selvedges, and two picks for weaving to the right relay and back to the selvedges. At each left relay, reverse the wefts around the same two warps. But at each right relay, advance the wefts one warp to the right.

Basic hatching technique worked in three degrees of value contrast: white and black, white and light gray, white and medium gray.

91

Slits will not be created in this example, since the butterflies relay at alternate positions every fourth row. Do not mark the warps; trust your eyes. The tips of the darker hatchings at the left form a vertical line. The lighter hatchings at the right become progressively longer, their tips forming a diagonal line.

Weave at least six hatchings. Then reverse the direction of the progression by shifting the relay at the right one warp to the left each time, creating progressively shorter hatchings. Weave at least six more hatchings.

Next, experience the interpretive freedom of this technique by creating a spontaneously designed example of irregular hatchings. Interrupt the rigid vertical line at the left; elongate the hatchings by moving both relays closer to the selvedges; shorten the hatchings by moving both relays farther away from the selvedges. End the darker butterfly at the completion of this example. Then, with the lighter butterfly, weave about ½″ of solid color to balance the border at the beginning of the example.

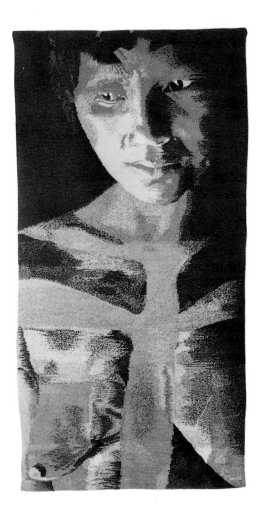

Tapestry by Brazilian Henrique Schucman, Mirada Indigena, 80″ x 40″ (200 x 100 cm.), 1987. Basic hatching as a shading technique.

Tips & Advice

Unique effects. The distinctive and very special characteristics of hatchings—patterns of slender, alternating fingers of contrasting colors—exist only in the art of tapestry weaving. Therefore, hatchings must be appreciated for their woven effects as well as for their potential for color interaction. Contrasting colors were chosen for this example to emphasize the woven effects of the hatching technique, especially its two very different possibilities for developing contours—one carefully controlled, the other irregular and spontaneous.

Opposing wefts. Adjacent contrasting wefts can be neatly and conveniently shifted to any position, every other row, only if they are traveling in opposite directions. For this reason, the technique of hatching, or any tapestry technique requiring frequent adjustments of the placement of weft colors, should be executed with opposing wefts.

Variations in technique. Observe the contour lines along the edges of the hatchings. It is here that you can vary the technique. The tips of the hatchings can be distributed along a vertical line, a diagonal line, or a vertical curve. And, as illustrated by the spontaneous example, hatchings of any length can evolve in a completely freeform manner with no obvious organization.

Design considerations. Hatchings may be introduced into a tapestry design to emphasize or echo its dominant lines and directions. Or hatchings can be used to soften or moderate certain contours. For example, if a tapestry design includes a certain straight vertical line that you wish to appear less rigid, consider hatching the two weft colors along the vertical line to soften and shade the juncture. Recall, too, that hatching eliminates slits, another justification for blending adjacent weft colors in this manner.

Variations in effect. The freeform experiment that modified the carefully controlled method of hatching to the more spontaneous placement of adjacent weft colors radically affected the woven and visual effects. The rigid precision of fine wavy lines metamorphosed into an expressive interpretation of an irregular contour. Shadings between weft colors hatched in an irregular manner are less formal—similar in effect to splashy layers of watercolors.

Hatching as Form Description
General Directions

Choose three colors of weft yarn: a light, a medium, and a dark value of one hue. For instance, if red is your chosen hue, the values should be light pink, medium red, and burgundy. Make two butterflies each with the dark-and middle-value yarns, and a single butterfly with the light one.

Next, imagine a simple oval shape, such as an egg or a cloud. This form will be created spontaneously by weaving irregular hatchings between the three weft colors. Two concentric contours, their edges shaded with inter-penetrating lines of weft color, will create a gently rounded oval image.

Into the next shed, enter one of the dark butterflies and weave about ten rows. Rest the butterfly at the left selvedge. Into the next shed, enter one of the middle-value butterflies at a point about 3″ from the right selvedge. Weave it toward the left to a point about 2″ from the left selvedge. Weave the resting butterfly to meet the new butterfly. Enter the other dark butterfly at the same point as the middle-value butterfly, and weave it to the right selvedge.

The area covered by the middle-value butterfly should be restricted to the approximate center of the weaving, while the two dark butterflies should travel only across the areas at the extreme left and right. However, both dark wefts should be hatched into the territory of the middle-value weft, and vice versa. Remember that hatching is created by shifting the relays of adjacent weft colors—which can only occur as butterflies travel toward each other. Therefore, the middle-value butterfly should relay in one shed with its neighbor to the left and in the opposite shed with its neighbor to the right. Weave about 12 rows, relaying and hatching. Then, to correctly position the wefts for the insertion of two additional colors, rest all three butterflies after they've been woven through the shed in which the middle-value butterfly traveled toward the left.

Change sheds and weave the dark butterfly at the right to a point about 2″ from the right selvedge. Enter the second middle-value butterfly at a point about 4″ from the right selvedge, and weave it toward the right, to meet the dark butterfly. Enter the lightest butterfly at the same point as the new middle-value butterfly, and weave it toward the left for about 1″. Weave the original middle-value butterfly toward the right to meet the lightest butterfly, and weave the remaining dark butterfly to the left selvedge. All five butterflies have thus been entered, and they are all traveling in opposition to one another.

Weave about 18 rows, manipulating the five butterflies in the same manner as the three. To describe the oval shape, first gradually expand, then gradually reduce, the width of the solid-color area in the center; the surrounding colors should flow freely around this shape. The light butterfly will relay alternately in opposite sheds with the two middle-value butterflies. Each middle-value butterfly will relay alternately with the light butterfly and a dark one. Create long hatchings between all five colors in a very expressive manner. The contours and shadings of this example should not appear calculated or intentionally symmetrical.

End the light butterfly and one of the middle-value butterflies in a row in which they travel toward each other. Overlap their tails over a lowered warp, and drop them to the back of the tapestry. Continue hatching with the remaining three butterflies for another 12 rows. Then, in the manner described above, end the middle-value butterfly and one of the dark butterflies. Complete the example with about ten rows of the dark weft color woven with the single remaining butterfly.

I have always believed and still believe that artists who live and work with spiritual values cannot and should not remain indifferent to a conflict in which the highest values of humanity and civilization are at stake.

—Pablo Picasso

93

Tips & Advice

Adding and deleting wefts. The technical challenge of weaving this section is to choreograph correctly the additions and deletions of wefts. Because certain tapestry techniques, such as hatching, can be executed only with wefts traveling in opposite directions, weaving with a single butterfly, adding additional pairs, and reversing the process are important skills to fully understand and refine.

Adding and deleting wefts in pairs helps you coordinate all involved butterflies. There are two procedures for entering an additional pair of butterflies into the middle of a row of weaving. The first, the simpler of the two, involves overlapping both tails of the new butterflies over a common lowered warp. This procedure works best if the new butterflies are the same color or if it does not matter whether the two colors become slightly mingled, as in this example. Occasionally, however, a pair of additional wefts must be entered in an uncluttered manner around adjacent warps. For instance, it may be necessary to enter two highly contrasting wefts at the bottom of a sharply defined vertical contour. In this case, the second procedure must be used, a procedure similar to the one for entering weft at a selvedge.

Entering a single additional weft color at either selvedge is never a problem, because it can be entered traveling in either direction. But consider the addition or deletion of a single butterfly from the middle of an established row of opposite-facing butterflies. This dilemma is conveniently solved by reversing the directions of all butterflies to one side or the other of the addition or deletion. To switch the direction of a butterfly, simply drop it through the warps at one edge of its weaving area and loop it across the reverse side of the tapestry to the opposite edge, where it can be woven through the shed from the opposite direction. Repeat the procedure as many times as necessary until all butterflies are traveling in opposition to one another. If you are weaving a tapestry from the reverse side, you can easily switch the direction of a butterfly by weaving it across its area from the opposite direction. In this case, the resulting loop faces the weaver.

Controlling the hatching lines. The artistic challenge of creating this intricately woven example is to effectively distribute the hatchings of five butterflies from eight directions. The light value is hatched in two directions; the two middle values are each hatched in two directions; and each of the dark values is hatched in one direction, for a total of eight possible hatching lines between the five butterflies. Described in these terms, the process may sound complicated, and the woven results certainly appear elaborate, but the spontaneous intermingling of five wefts will prove to be such an enjoyable and undemanding experience that you will probably look forward to experimenting even further with the possibilities of this technique.

Design considerations. As you watch the evolution of the woven effects of this technique, note the proportions of the three colors and their relative positions within the design. In this example, the darkest hatchings contribute a great deal of visual weight. The careless placement of this element in an actual tapestry could overwhelm its design. Would you prefer to see this design with different proportions of the three weft colors, perhaps reducing one of the colors to an absolute minimum? How would

Introducing a new weft between two wefts traveling in opposite directions.

you like to distribute your hatchings in future tapestry designs? How would you adjust the combination of weft colors? Based on your observations of this example, which woven effects do you consider most succesful or least successful?

Visual effects. Step away from the loom to observe the hatchings from a greater distance. Do there appear to be more than three colors in the example? These illusory half-tones are the result of optical blends in the hatched areas between adjacent colors. And the effect is further enhanced by the strong hue relationship between the three values. Consider using three weft yarns with even more closely related hues, values, and intensities. In this case, a nearly flawless modulation could be achieved.

Adding colors. The hatching technique could be expanded horizontally to include more than three colors of weft. As always, consider the scale of the tapestry, the scale of the shaded area in relation to the size of the tapestry, the scale of the woven texture as determined by warp/weft proportions, and the distance from which the tapestry will be viewed.

Additional effects. Simple hatching can be expanded to include additional woven effects. Consider the possibility of adding dotted areas to one extreme of the gradation. This could be very effective, extending the shaded effect even further. Or loop wefts across the back of the tapestry to shift colors around at will or to instinctively create contrasting lines or dots.

Reversing values. Consider how the example might appear if the positions of the three values of wefts were reversed. Surrounded by progressively darker colors, the lightest color seems to be lifted out of a shadow. Reversing the values in the gradation would similarly reverse the dimensional effect.

A source of light in a woven design could be expressed by a careful distribution of light, middle, and dark values, blended with hatchings to create a gradual modulation.

Plausible depth of space within a tapestry design can be created with hatched shadings. In this case, both intensity and value must be carefully modulated.

Uses. Simple hatching is an especially valuable tool for tapestry weavers, as it can be used to create both horizontal and vertical gradations. And, as illustrated by the execution of this simple example, by carefully controlling the distribution of the involved colors, a weaver can even create the appearance of a circular gradation.

Personal expression. If the hatchings between the three wefts were intentionally regular in size and placement, the result would be a very different style of expression. Perhaps you prefer a more organized approach. Look through the book and examine the shading techniques used by a world of weavers; do you have strong feelings about certain techniques?

Vertical curved lines. Consider the effects of hatching along a vertical curved line. Remember that as the degree of its angle is changed, a vertical curved line may develop an uneven quality, including all of the following characteristics: high steps, low steps, bumpy angles, smooth angles, and slits. You can use simple hatchings between the two wefts to break the sharply defined contours of the two weft colors and to make the curved line uniform, with no slits.

I would hope that my works could last for many centuries, and this is why I hand-dye my yarns and use the Gobelin technique.

—Joyce Hulbert

95

Triangular Hachures

General Directions

Choose two weft yarns with contrasting hues and values, and make a butterfly with each.

Enter the lighter butterfly into the next shed at either selvedge, and weave about ten rows, creating a solid-color border. Rest this butterfly at the left selvedge.

Into the next shed, enter the darker butterfly at the right selvedge, and weave it to a point about 3″ from the left selvedge. Change sheds, reverse the direction of the butterfly, and weave it back to the right selvedge. These two picks are the first step of a three-step hachure. To weave picks three and four, again weave the darker butterfly toward the left selvedge to a new relay position, six warps to the right of the previous relay. Continue this pattern for a total of eight picks. In other words, the darker butterfly should be woven for eight picks in succession, while the lighter butterfly rests. Each of the four relays made by the darker butterfly should be six warps to the right of the previous relay. Observe the exaggerated triangular shape, with its equally graded steps.

Next, weave eight picks with the lighter butterfly, meeting the relays of the darker butterfly, step by step. Four times, the lighter butterfly will advance to each successive step, relay around the warp to its left, and return to the left selvedge. The weaving of these eight picks should result in a second triangle, inverted over the first.

Build a series of ten hachures (five triangles of each weft color). Eight picks (four complete passes) of each weft color are required for each pair of opposing triangles. Since the triangles are woven with identical relays, they develop in an orderly, precise manner, their points forming vertical lines. End the darker butterfly at the right selvedge, and weave a narrow border over the example with the lighter butterfly. Rest the lighter butterfly at the left selvedge.

Observe the hachures. Because you wove the example with contrasting colors, the triangles, the steps, and the overall pattern are obvious. The next example demonstrates two other important aspects of triangular hachures: their extraordinary effectiveness when placed along a diagonal contour, and their uncanny ability to approximate intermediate colors between the wefts involved.

Choose a color of weft yarn, closely related in hue and value to the color of the butterfly resting at the left selvedge, and make a butterfly with this new weft yarn.

This time the hachures should follow imaginary diagonal lines, moving first toward the left, then toward the right. With the butterfly at the left selvedge, weave an eight-row hachure, placing its point (first relay) about 3″ from the right selvedge. Each step of this hachure should be six warps to the left of the previous relay. Next, enter the new butterfly at the right selvedge, and weave eight corresponding rows. Weave another eight-row hachure with the butterfly at the left; this time, carefully shift all four of its relays two warps to the left. Again, weave eight corresponding rows with the butterfly at the right. Continue weaving in this manner, building a series of eight hachures (four triangles of each weft color), each step of each one shifted two warps to the left.

Next, reverse the procedure by shifting the position of each hachure two warps to the right. Build another series of eight hachures (four triangles of

Triangular hachures woven on a sett of 6 epi, with a very high degree of contrast and with closely related values.

each weft color), moving toward the right selvedge. End the new butterfly at the right selvedge. Continue weaving with the original butterfly for 1″ more, creating a border over this section. End the butterfly at either selvedge.

Observe the rhythm of the pattern created by the hachures and the gentle echoes created by the precise diagonal positions of the steps along the triangles. Shifting each relay in the same direction and by the same increment ensures an orderly procession of hachures. This rhythm and orderliness enhance the potential for achieving an optical blend between the two weft colors. Stand at least five feet away from your loom and observe the shimmering, shaded effect in the hatched area.

Tips & Advice

Variations. Both of these examples are the classic spear-shaped hachure, used for centuries in tapestry weaving. But this formula is by no means the only one. Understanding the basic theories behind this device provides unlimited possibilities for creating shadings, gradations, progressions, and stylizations. Consider the visual elements involved and their numerous variations.

1. Element number one is the size of the hachures. You, the weaver/designer, determine their size, based on the scale of the tapestry, the scale of the shaded area, and the specific visual effect you desire.

For instance, the Coptic weavers wove very short, sharply pointed triangles, constructed over eccentric wefts. These hachures emphasized and outlined a darker area, while merging it into a lighter area. A slightly shaded effect occurred between the weft colors, but the small-scale, stylized images remained essentially two-dimensional.

On the other hand, the Gothic weavers wove long, exaggerated, regularly spaced spears between two or three wefts of contrasting values or hues. When viewed from a distance, the effect was a richly shaded surface, describing rounded forms.

These two very different interpretations of hachures were, in both instances, appropriate to the scale of the tapestry and thus visually successful. Moreover, these distinctive applications reflected the prevailing styles and techniques of each particular culture.

When planning the size of hachures for your tapestries, consider the width and length of the shaded area, to help you determine the correct scale. Then consider the woven effect you wish to achieve. Short, sharply pointed hachures are developed over a narrow width; they are more emphatic but less elegant. Longer hachures require a wider space within the tapestry, but they appear finer in scale, evolving into a subtle linear pattern.

2. Element number two is the steps along the side of the triangle. First, consider the number of steps (you could plan two or four, instead of my assigned three). Then consider the width of the steps (you could shift eight, nine, ten warps, etc., instead of my assigned six). Consider also the possibility of building steps along both sides of the triangles (this works only with a fine weft woven on a closely sett warp). Finally, consider the precision of the steps (you could vary the widths of the steps, intentionally breaking their strict geometric pattern).

In general, triangular hachures introduce a formal, orderly style of shading, which reflects the precision within the hachures themselves.

Triangular hachures woven on a sett of 10 epi.

3. Element number three is the colors involved, more specifically, their hues, values, intensities, and temperatures. As with most tapestry techniques, successful hachures depend upon appropriate and well-planned contrasts between weft colors.

It has long been thought that hachures were originally conceived to cleverly compensate for a weaver's limited range of available hues and values of weft yarns. By compelling two values of a hue to pierce each other from opposing directions at regular intervals, an intermediate tone was created—a result of the optical blend within the hatched area.

Look closely at a newspaper illustration. The simplest element is used—a tiny black dot. But by skillfully organizing millions of these dots on white paper, printers can create intricate shadings and gradations with which to describe forms, light source, and depth of space.

Fragment of a Coptic hanging with a hunting scene; 6th-century Egypt. Slit tapestry over one warp, triangular hachures. Warp of undyed wool, weft of dyed wool: red, pink, green, blue, brown, beige, tan, yellow, and rust. Collection of the Textile Museum, Washington, D.C.

The same visual principles apply to hachures—a uniform element of a specific and carefully chosen scale, repeated in a regular pattern and viewed from a distance. Hachures function quite successfully between contrasting hues and values if they are handled skillfully and if a bold, graphic visual effect is desired.

On the other hand, hachures can also interpret delicate, subtle shadings if the involved weft colors are closely related in hue and value. Viewed at a distance, closely related hachures look like gently rippled modulations. Therefore, the ultimate character of the hachures is greatly influenced by color relationships. Consult the examples in the illustrations. Use these as the basis for your own experimentation, and find the color relationships and style of hachure that best express your designs.

Basic Weft-Blending Technique

General Directions

To provide a valuable record of the three distinct variations within this technique, weave the examples with two highly contrasting colors of weft yarn. Black and white, or two extremes of hue and value, would be most effective. While sharply contrasting colors cannot blend optically, they can impressively demonstrate the distinctive nuances of each variation.

Make a single butterfly using an equal number of strands of both colors of weft yarn. With it, weave at least 1″. Do not attempt to control the placement of the weft colors. As the yarn is pulled from the butterfly, it may twist slightly. Frequently, the two colors will be distributed horizontally through the shed, one above the other. As you build row upon row, observe the slightly mottled, hit-or-miss texture and the pronounced horizontal lines. Compare these razor-sharp lines with the wavy ones created by weaving contrasting colors into opposite sheds. An idiosyncrasy such as this is not to be overlooked. It may prove to be a useful tool at some point.

With the same butterfly, weave another 1″. This time, before bubbling and beating each row, gently twist the wefts together once or twice. Note that the pronounced horizontal lines of the first example have been eliminated in the second. Also observe the marblelike pattern created by twisting the wefts.

Weave a third example of the same size, using the same weft colors. This time, before beating each row, place the darker weft above the lighter one. An orderly and consistent arrangement of the two weft colors results in an even texture of a very small scale.

Next, choose three colors of weft yarn with closely related hues and values. Perhaps you have three slightly contrasting values of blue, or three light, compatible greens. Make a single butterfly containing an equal number of strands of all three weft colors.

With this harmonious but more complicated weft blend, repeat the variations. The woven and color effects of these examples will be quite different. The three related weft colors should blend visually, producing mellow, shimmering textures instead of bold patterns, and velvety vertical shadings instead of horizontal lines. These are truly extraordinary tools for tapestry interpretations.

A trick for evaluating the relative weights (sizes) of two weft blends.

Tips & Advice

Blended effects. Blending more than one color of weft yarn through a shed significantly alters the character of the weave. Compare a woven surface constructed with a single color of weft with that of a blended weft. The former looks like a solid area of clear color, constructed with a uniform texture. The latter is created with tiny angled strokes of contrasting colors or small-scale textures, resulting in distinctively handwoven effects and colors of unusual complexity and richness.

The weaver as pointillist. By describing shapes on their canvasses with myriad tiny dots, pointillist painters create color in the eye of the viewer. Observed at close range, these dots are clearly individual contrasting colors. But viewed from a distance, they blend optically to create shimmering intermediate tones. A tapestry provides the perfect opportunity for exploiting these pointillist color effects. With a single woven pick, blended wefts provide an entire row of tiny contrasting specks of color. Then, as if by magic, new colors seem to wash over the yarns, colors related to the individual elements, but richer and livelier.

Weft blends versus dyes. Tapestry weavers can also use the principles of pointillism to cleverly create additional weft colors without resorting to dyes. For instance, light peach, light beige, and off-white could blend to create a lively, warm neutral color. Light violet, light orange, and light gray could blend to create a soft, rosy color. Manufacture a sparkling, less weighty black by blending flat black with darkest violet or navy blue. Blended weft colors may actually prove to be more successful than solid-color custom-dyed yarns. Always evaluate blended effects from a distance. Step back from your loom, observe the optical blends under various lighting conditions, and train your eyes to reject any unsuccessful contrasts.

A single strand. The assigned warp/weft proportions for this sampler permit a wide variety of experiments in color blending. For instance, a five-or six-strand butterfly may include several different but closely related hues with which to create subtle shadings. Or experiment with adding a single fine strand of a contrasting color to a weft blend to create elusive textural effects. I have had great success with blended wefts that include a strand or two of mercerized cotton embroidery floss, or a fine strand of gold or silver metallic thread. A single strand of a very light or lustrous yarn can add additional shimmer and highlight to a weft blend of a light value.

Three-strand wools. There are two completely different methods for blending wefts with three-strand, Persian-type wools. If a weft blend requires two or three strands of a single color, and those strands remain clumped together in the blend, that color appears in the weave as a bold stroke. To fragment the weight and strength of an individual weft while retaining the proportions of the blended colors, separate the individual strands of wool. Finer, single strands mingle with the other weft colors in a less obtrusive manner.

Unity of design. Blended wefts can be used to establish subliminal color relationships within a tapestry design. By including a strand of a common color in several weft blends throughout the tapestry, you introduce a subtle but most effective unifying element. Recognized principles guiding two-dimensional art require that critical contrasts in a design be resolved with a quantitative dominance of a single, important visual element. Therefore, the frequent reiteration of a certain weft color can provide significant harmony to a design for tapestry.

Transparency. Blended wefts can be used to create an illusion of transparency. For example, two blends of weft colors might be used to describe a glass of juice on a table. One blend, which would include the colors of the table and the colors of the glass, would be used for the empty portion of the glass. The other blend, including the colors of the juice and the colors of the glass, would be used for the filled portion of the glass. Additional shadings of the color of the glass would be added to describe its opaque edges and rims.

Color. Tapestry colors created with blended weft yarns are extraordinarily deep and rich. These very special and singularly handwoven effects more than compensate for any vexations encountered handling weaving materials. As with any other technique, experimentation expands your frame of reference. Weave samples exploring relationships between weft colors. Form opinions about the success or failure of certain weft blends. And begin to develop highly personal tapestry interpretations by selecting from the infinite possibilities those most relevant to your particular style.

Weft blending. Some general rules of thumb to guide your experiments in the blending of weft colors are:

1. Strong hue and value contrasts do not blend optically; rather, they appear as textures in the weave.
2. Weft colors of minimal hue or value contrast result in the smoothest optical blends.
3. Two weft colors with a moderate degree of hue or value contrast should mingle harmoniously when viewed from a moderate distance, especially if a weft color of a third, intermediate hue or value is added to the blend.
4. Complementary hue contrasts—such as red/green, violet/yellow, and blue/orange—can blend to produce a lively neutral tone if you choose similar values of these hues (use a very light violet with yellow) and extremely fine strands. In addition, a neutral strand (gray or beige of the same value) will contribute a clever modulating factor.
5. Darkest black and brightest white tend to dominate any blend of weft colors in which they are included. Warm beiges or cool grays combine more successfully with hues or other neutrals.
6. Hues that are similar in temperature harmonize most successfully. For instance, cool colors, such as blue-green and blue-violet, blend optically if their values are similar. Closely related warm colors, such as rust and burgundy, blend beautifully, resulting in a much more interesting dark red area than either color used singly.
7. Keep in mind that all colors are relative. A light pastel color appears relatively lighter used with a very dark color, while the same pastel may seem shaded next to pure white. A warm rose appears hot next to an icy blue and cooler next to bright pink. Dull brown becomes even more drab combined with vivid turquoise but may appear warm and lively used with soft blue.

Eight examples of weft blends, worked in various hues, temperatures, and values. Some blends involve only two colors, others as many as six.

A weft-blended gradation between extremes of value, hue, and intensity.

Creating Gradations With Weft Blends

General Directions

Choose two weft yarns of the same hue with a moderate degree of value contrast. Robin's-egg blue and medium blue would be appropriate choices, or peach and orange, or white and medium gray. Cut several three-yard (2.7-meter) lengths of both weft colors; separate the individual strands if the weft is three-strand Persian wool, and make nine three-yard butterflies using the following proportions.

Butterfly #1: five strands of the darker weft and one strand of the lighter weft.

Butterfly #2: four strands of the darker weft and two strands of the lighter weft.

Butterfly #3: three strands of each weft.

Butterfly #4: two strands of the darker weft and four strands of the lighter weft.

Butterfly #5: one strand of the darker weft and five strands of the lighter weft.

Butterfly #6: two strands of the darker weft and four strands of the lighter weft.

Butterfly #7: three strands of each weft.

Butterfly #8: four strands of the darker weft and two strands of the lighter weft.

Butterfly #9: five strands of the darker weft and one strand of the lighter weft.

If a six-strand butterfly is too heavy for your circumstances, use the same theory to make seven five-strand butterflies. Number the butterflies in some manner, arrange them in order, and observe the beautiful gradation already in progress, moving from dark to light and back again.

Begin weaving from selvedge to selvedge with butterfly #1. After you've woven about ½″, weave butterfly #1 from the left selvedge to a point about 1″ from the left selvedge. Enter butterfly #2 at the right selvedge, and weave it to meet butterfly #1. Change sheds and return both butterflies to their original selvedges.

Change sheds again and weave butterfly #1 to a point about 1″ from the right selvedge. Weave butterfly #2 to the same relay point, change sheds, and again return both butterflies to their original selvedges. Observe that you've woven two very long hatchings with the slightly contrasting butterflies. The purpose of these hatchings is to create an imperceptible transition between the first and second butterflies. Continue weaving irregular hatchings between the two colors, relaying the butterflies at any point along the row of weaving. When butterfly #1 is depleted, end it at the left selvedge. Butterfly #2 may then travel from selvedge to selvedge.

Repeat the procedure with all nine (or seven) butterflies. First weave with a single butterfly traveling from selvedge to selvedge until about ½″ of that color has been woven. Then begin its gradual exodus while progressively introducing the next color in the sequence. The weaving of this example produces two gradations: The first progresses from a darker to a lighter value; the second is an inversion of the first.

Tips & Advice

Subtlety. This dynamic woven technique has intentionally been placed at the end of this chapter, because it is the ultimate refinement of shading with colors of weft yarns. Weft-blended gradations are the most subtle of all tapestry-shading techniques. If they have been gradually introduced, the individual steps blend smoothly into one another.

Design considerations. Experiment to determine how much contrast can be modulated with this technique. (To "modulate" is to move gradually, in small successive steps, between contrasting elements.) Consider such factors as the distance and angle from which the tapestry will be viewed, the size of the gradation compared to the size of the tapestry, and the strength of the other contrasts in the tapestry.

Extreme values. To weave a gradation between even greater extremes of value, use more than two values of yarn. For instance, black and white cannot be modulated without several intervening values of gray. There will be more steps between the two extremes, of course, and the size of the intervals may also require adjustment.

Applications. The theory of adjusting the proportions of values in weft blends also applies to gradations between other color characteristics. For instance, the intensity of a hue can be gradually lowered by introducing a series of weft blends with progressively greater proportions of a less intense hue. This type of gradation may or may not express a shift of value as well. If you modulate both intensity and value in the same gradation, you can portray depth of space very effectively.

Or plan a gradation between two hues—say, from soft violet to soft orange. Try including a single strand of a middle value neutral in each weft blend to function as a modulating element.

Color theory. Learning to select and successfully combine weft colors is as important as acquiring perfectly refined tapestry-weaving skills. Learning about hues and their relative intensities and temperatures usually becomes a lifelong, pleasurable pursuit for weavers/designers, while selecting successful value contrasts and applying them appropriately becomes their greatest aesthetic challenge.

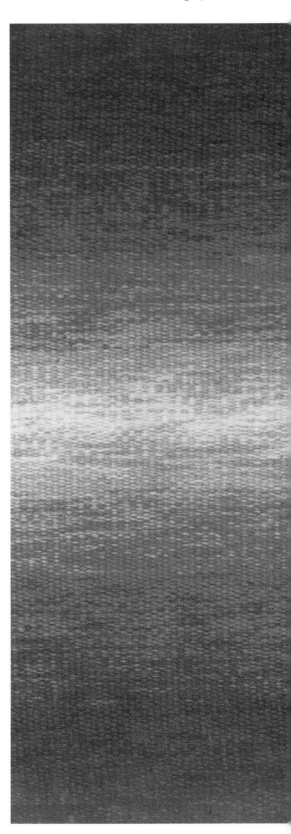

A gradation between extremes of value: black to white with several intermediate grays.

The nine butterflies required for creating the gradation of weft blends described in the text. Photographed by George Goodwin.

103

Bessarabian Rug. Two-ply wool warp, single-spun wool weft; 68″ x 41″ (170 by 103 cm.). Photo: George Mauro. Collection of Jason Nazmiyal/Rug & Kilim. Woven dots, eccentric wefts, dynamic hachures, two-color weft twining.

Aubusson Tapestry. Two-ply silk warp, single-spun silk weft; 240″ x 264″ (600 by 660 cm.). Photo: George Mauro. Collection of Jason Nazmiyal/Rug & Kilim. Hachures, vertical curved lines, sewn slits.

Bessarabian Rug (detail).

SHADING TECHNIQUES

105

Julia Mitchell, Green Jungle. Linen warp, wool weft; 42" x 30" (105 by 75 cm.); 1980. Eccentric wefts, transparent top and bottom borders.

Elaine Ireland, Amazon Lilies. Woven by the artist, Susan Hart Henegar, and Susan Marvin. Cotton warp, wool weft with silk threads, 48" x 192" in three panels (120 by 480 cm.); 1982. Photo: Don Beatty.

Julia Mitchell, Cedar Tree Neck II. Linen warp, wool weft; 36″ x 48″ (90 by 120 cm.); 1988. Photo: Bruno Debas.

Cedar Tree Neck II (detail).

SHADING TECHNIQUES

Barbara Heller, Passages. Linen warp, wool weft, some hand-spun, all hand-dyed; 45″ x 60″ (113 by 150 cm.); 1987. Photo: Barbara Cohen. Collection of Mrs. Drumheller.

Michelle Lester, Ruwenzori Jungle. Woven by Michelle Lester Studio Weavers. Wool warp and weft; 48″ x 96″ (120 by 240 cm.); 1987. Photo: Gustavo Gonzalez.

Regine Bartsch, With You. *Linen warp, silk and wool weft; 40″ x 80″ (100 by 200 cm.); 1987.*

Linda Hutchins, Beth's Door. *Linen warp; wool, goat hair, and linen weft; 32″ x 22½″ (80 by 56 cm.); 1988.*

Constance Hunt, The Red Nude. *Cotton warp, wool weft; 48″ x 35″ (120 by 88 cm.); 1984. Photo: Gary Hunt.*

Tricia Goldberg and Bonni Boren, Untitled Abstract. *Woven by Tricia Goldberg. Cotton warp, wool weft; 57″ x 44″ (143 by 110 cm.); 1987. Photo: Bruce Handelsman.*

SHADING TECHNIQUES

Henrique Schucman, Cidadindio ("City Indian"); 120" x 80" (300 by 200 cm.); 1986-87. Alto-lico (high-warp).

Judy Chicago, The Creation of the World (detail). Woven by Audrey Cowan. 42" x 14' (105 cm. by 4.25 m.); 1984. Photo: Michele Maier.

Micala Sidore, The Pleasant Street Theater.
Wool warp and weft; 28″ x 32″ (70 by 80 cm.);
1983. Collection of John and Julie Morrison.

Victor Jacoby, Shadows on the Road Home.
Cotton warp, wool weft; 29″ x 31″ (73 by 78
cm.); 1989. Photo by James D. Toms.

112

Eccentric Wefts

"Eccentric" wefts deviate to some degree from their usual perpendicular relationship to the warps. Easily identifiable by their angled or undulating appearance in the weave, eccentric wefts gracefully describe rounded shapes or softly curved lines. This sensuous and expressive tapestry technique has been practiced since ancient times, most notably by the Coptic weavers of Egypt from the third to early seventh centuries A.D. Historians have discovered that, in the days of the early Egyptian Christians, it was customary for weavers to embellish the necklines, sleeves, or hems of plain weave garments with inserted areas of colorful tapestry. Because these garments were buried on their owners, they have been preserved for centuries in the dry sands of Egypt, allowing us to document a profound technical link between ancient and contemporary tapestry weavers.

As you weave the examples of eccentric wefts in this chapter, you will also experiment with a different method of design interpretation. Thus far, most of the tapestry sampler has been planned to be woven one complete row at a time, while relaying or crossing a butterfly for each color area between the selvedges. The next two sections introduce the exciting possibility of interpreting tapestry designs in sequentially woven sections. While most of the techniques discussed in the book could be successfully applied to either style of weaving, eccentric wefts, because of their digression from horizontally woven rows, may be used only on tapestries developed section by section.

Many weavers prefer interpreting designs one small area at a time even when they haven't included eccentric wefts, just for the luxury of focusing on the development of one specific element. Imagine the creative satisfaction of executing an elegant leaf, fully resolving its complicated shadings and delicate veins before proceeding with the weaving of an adjacent flower or the background over the leaf.

Three Eccentric Ovals

General Directions

Select a weft yarn for weaving the background of this example—any color, but with a very light value. Make two butterflies. Then select three darker, contrasting weft colors, or blends of colors, for weaving the oval shapes. Creating two of the shapes with blended wefts and the third with a solid-color weft will set up an interesting comparison between blended and solid-color areas. Make a butterfly with each of these three weft colors or blends.

Enter the two background butterflies into the next shed, traveling in opposite directions. With these butterflies, weave a solid-color background 1″ (2.5 cm.) wide. This is the base upon which the first oval shape will be developed. Rest the two butterflies at the selvedges.

The beginning of the development of the eccentric oval shape.

Expanding the oval shape in both directions. The extra length of white yarn is inserted to correct the shed to the left of the oval.

The resolution of the oval insert: its rounded top.

For the background weft to travel from selvedge to selvedge, the shed must again be corrected from the top of the oval to the right selvedge.

Enter one of the contrasting butterflies around a lowered warp, about 2″ (5 cm.) to the left of the center of the sampler. With this butterfly traveling in either direction, weave about six short picks, back and forth over four warps, beating with a hand beater. Then, to create a rounded oval shape, gradually increase the width of this area every row, by advancing the weft one or two warps in both directions.

At this point, you should encounter an unfamiliar technical dilemma: uncoordinated sheds. Note that, as the butterfly is woven toward one of the selvedges, the shed is the correct one for advancing the color in that direction. But as the butterfly is woven toward the opposite selvedge, the shed is the incorrect one for advancing the color in that direction. To resolve this dilemma, cut a short length of weft yarn the color of the background. Change sheds, and lay this weft across the incorrect shed next to the oval insert for about 2″, its tails tucked to the reverse side of the tapestry. When the shed is switched for weaving the next row, the incorrect segment will be adjusted, allowing the contrasting weft to be correctly advanced in both directions.

When the oval insert measures about 2″ wide, begin to decrease its width gradually until it eventually becomes a point. End the butterfly by wrapping it around the last warp and securing its tail over a nearby lowered warp. Study the elliptical shape created by increasing, then decreasing, the width of the woven rows.

Open the shed for weaving the next row, and adjust any uncoordinated segments. Weave the butterfly at the left selvedge about halfway across the width of the sampler. With a hand beater, carefully pack the background yarn into the shed, following the curved line. Change sheds, reverse the direction of the butterfly, and weave it back to the left selvedge. Continue in this manner, completely surrounding the oval with about eight picks of background weft. To avoid creating a slit, reverse the direction of the weft around a different warp each time. Again, rest the background butterfly at the left selvedge.

Look closely at the fluid rows of background weft as they travel over the oval. By forcing wefts to deviate from their strictly perpendicular relationship to the warp, you create eccentric wefts. Their oblique position in the shed introduces variations of texture, direction, and line while expanding the possibilities for design interpretation.

Enter another of the contrasting butterflies about 1″ to the right of the bottom of the hill. Make any necessary shed adjustment, and create a second oval insert. Be very free and creative as you develop this asymmetrical oval, allowing its bottom curve to conform to that of the existing background contour.

When the second oval has been completed to your satisfaction, the butterfly should be near its top. Do not end the butterfly; weave it along one side of the oval to meet the background. Change sheds, reverse the direction of the butterfly, and weave it to meet the background at the opposite side of the oval. Continue weaving in the same direction, laying 2″ or 3″ (3.5 cm.) of contrasting weft over the background. Again change sheds, reverse the direction of the butterfly, and weave it back to the opposite side of the oval. At this point, end the butterfly. You have outlined the oval with its own color, further softening and defining its curved contour. And with the same continuous weft, you have also created a fine, curved line bleeding into the background from the edge of the oval. The curve of this line will be emphasized as background weft is subsequently woven over it.

With the background butterfly at the right selvedge, weave about four rows over the second oval. Retain the curve between the two inserts, since the third oval will be developed in this valley. Rest the background butterfly at the right selvedge.

Enter the third contrasting butterfly 1″ from the right selvedge. Weave it toward the left into the valley between the two inserts. The reason for this very long first row is to create a delicate curve of tiny dots, bleeding from the right edge of the third oval. Weaving back and forth in the valley, create another oval in the same manner as the first two. Ignore, for now, the single row of weft flowing from its right edge. As background weft is woven over this single row, it will become a row of dots. End the butterfly when the third oval has been completed.

Adjust the shed as necessary and fill in the background areas, weaving with each of the background butterflies as required. Weave short rows in the valleys, meeting the sides of the hills with background weft. Eventually, the background should be level with the top of the third oval. This straight row may then be beaten with the loom beater. Weave about 1″ of background above the third oval, completing this example.

Tips & Advice

Spontaneity. For the most part, this example should be designed as you weave; exact measurements are not important. Since you are weaving a freeform design, you cannot make an error in the placement or size of the ovals. It is more important to develop a feel for weaving in this manner and to understand the methodology. More than any other, this tapestry technique requires sensitivity to the weft materials. Mold the oval shapes with your fingers, and use the point of a tapestry bobbin or a blunt needle to refine the contour.

Incorrect sheds. As you develop shapes and background areas independently, weaving sheds will become uncoordinated. For instance, you may wish to place background weft over a contrasting shape and its adjacent background areas. But, as you open the correct shed for weaving over one of the background areas, you discover that the contrasting shape and the other background area are both in the incorrect shed. This is an easy problem to solve. Simply cut a short length of weft yarn, switch to the previous shed, and lay the weft over the segment requiring adjustment. When the weaving shed is open, all segments should be in the correct shed. The color of the yarn inserted can relate to either the shape or the background, or you can introduce a row of dots in a contrasting color if you wish. Direct the tails of the short length of weft to the reverse side of the tapestry.

Going too far. It is impossible to weave eccentric wefts around very steep curves. If wefts are forced to deviate too greatly from their optimum perpendicular relationship to the warp, the textile may become distorted or structurally weak. In addition, wefts that are excessively eccentric, traveling upward between two warps for too great a distance, may appear in the woven texture as overshots or mistakes. A very steep hill (greater than 45°) should be met row by row with background weft, moving logically from warp to warp.

Contrasting effects. Observe the two curved rows of contrasting wefts bleeding into the background. One is a solid line, woven with two rows; the other is a single row, resulting in tiny dots. These accents result from entering or ending an inserted eccentric weft color in a creative manner. You can plan eccentric accents as subtle or emphatic as you wish.

The equation that one tapestry weaver equals five sheep has a certain ecological attractiveness. The annual shearing from five such beasts will provide the weft yarn for the 100 or so square feet (ten square metres) that is the approximate yearly output of a busy tapestry weaver.

—Archie Brennan

Bubbling. More attention is required to bubble the correct amount of weft into a curved row of weaving. Try using the point of a tapestry bobbin for packing weft around hills and valleys. Lay the weft yarn loosely across the shed, and tuck it around the curve with the point of the bobbin. I frequently use only my fingers for packing eccentric wefts, determining by my touch the precise amount of weft yarn for following a curve. Another of my favorite tools is a handsome, antique-ivory lace bobbin with a long tapered end, indispensable for packing very fine tapestries.

Design. Vary the sizes of the three oval shapes, as well as the intervals of negative space around them. These are basic design principles, and it would be helpful to become familar with them. (Several books on two-dimensional design are included in the bibliography.) Tapestries are time-consuming to weave. A skillfully designed cartoon successfully communicates your special insights and responses, making every moment of weaving worthwhile.

Pitfalls and Solutions

The life so short,

the craft so long to learn.

—Hippocrates

Pitfall: An unwoven area buried underneath a woven area.
Solution: Weave first any sections sloping upward toward a selvedge. Remind yourself never to weave over unwoven warps.

Pitfall: Uncoordinated sheds.
Solution: Insert lengths of weft as required, adjusting any incorrect segments.

Pitfall: Selvedges bulging outward.
Solution: Never use the loom beater for packing narrow areas, even if they are accessible. To do so packs excess weft into the area, causing the warps to spread.
    Another cause of bulging selvedges may be eccentric wefts that are too steep. Excessively steep wefts float upward between the warps at too great an angle, distorting the woven texture.

Pitfall: Selvedges drawing inward.
Solution: Pack eccentric wefts very carefully around curves. Remember that weft must travel a greater distance around a curve than across a straight line.

Pitfall: Uncovered warps.
Solution: These may be caused by double weft in a shed. Adjust any incorrect segments before weaving the row.

Pitfall: The tapestry puckers in certain areas when it is released from tension.
Solution: This is usually caused by weaving with wefts of unequal weights. Make each butterfly with the same number of strands, or with strands of comparable weight.

116

Mountains and Valleys

General Directions

Choose five colors of weft yarn for weaving the design, and make a butterfly with each. Sections one and five, indicated on the cartoon, should be woven with solid weft colors, contrasting sharply with each other in hue, value, or both. Sections two, three, and four should be woven with blends of weft colors. Relate a strand of yarn in each blend to one of the solid-color sections or to one of the other blends. In other words, the colors of the solid and blended areas should communicate with each other in some manner. It should be interesting to compare the visual textures of the juxtaposed solid and blended color areas and to evaluate the effect they have on one another.

Trace the contour lines from the cartoon on page 118 onto heavy tracing paper. Using two large spring clips or T-pins, fasten the tracing paper to the warps at the selvedges, carefully positioning line A along the fell. With the cartoon temporarily placed in correct relationship to the warps, transcribe the contour lines for sections one and two by placing tiny dots onto the warps directly above the line on the cartoon. Remove the cartoon and extend each dot to completely surround the warp (remember to use a permanent marker).

At point W, enter the butterfly to be used for weaving section one. Weave this butterfly toward the left selvedge. Following the marked warps, continue weaving section one, row by row. Beating carefully with a hand beater, cover each successive dot with weft yarn. A steep (45° or greater) curve such as this should be developed with horizontal rows of weaving. To force wefts into the shed at such an angle would not only look messy but could seriously compromise the quality of the tapestry. End the first butterfly after completing the gently curved mound at the top of the hill. You have now woven section one in its entirety, completely independent of the other four shapes.

At point W, enter the butterfly to be used for weaving section two, and weave it toward the right selvedge. Begin weaving section two, meeting the curved edge of section one, row by row. Observe that each weft turn in section two correctly meets and overlaps the rows of section one. Because the two butterflies were entered to travel in opposite directions, all weft relays occur in the correct shed, just as they would if the two sections were woven simultaneously. There are two low hills at the top of section two. Weave the left hill first, continuing to meet the curve of section one at the left while following the dots describing the top of section two at the right. Then carry the butterfly through the shed to the right selvedge, and focus on the development of the other hill. Create its rounded top while building a straight selvedge as usual. To further define the curves along the top of section two, line B may be outlined with two or more rows of eccentric wefts. End the butterfly at point X.

At this point, it is necessary to transcribe the remaining lines from the cartoon onto the warps. As you position the cartoon under the warps this time, compare the lines on the paper with the woven lines. Do not expect perfection. Look for equality of volume and angle between the cartoon and the woven shapes, not identical lines. Trace lines C and D. Remove the cartoon, and extend the dots around the warps.

The correct direction for entering a new weft adjacent to a previously woven area.

Entering a new weft into an uncoordinated shed: traveling first in one direction to bring that portion of the row into coordination with the other, then in the other direction, traveling cleanly across the entire row.

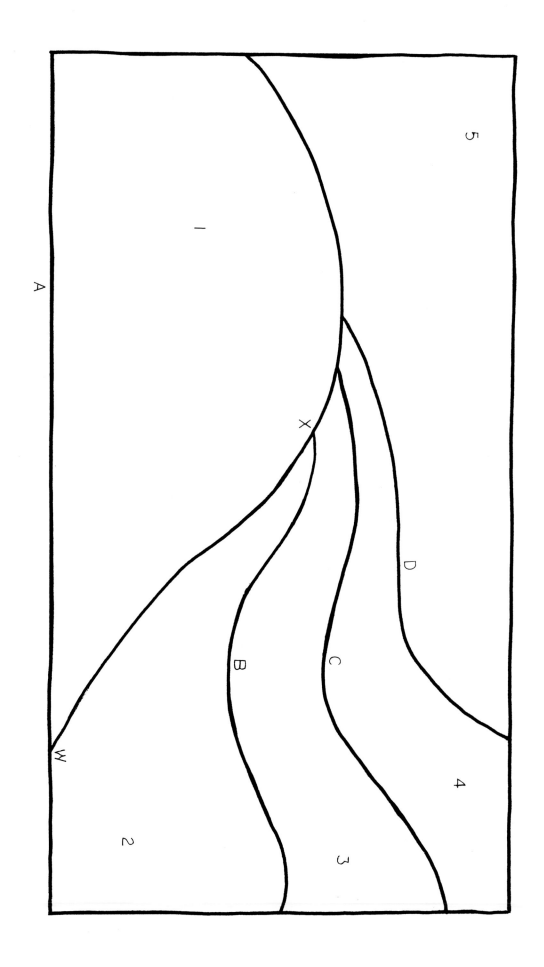

Next weave section three. The butterfly to be used for this section must travel over two previously woven sections, so check the weaving shed and make any necessary adjustments. Because the curves of lines B and C are less than 45°, section three may be woven entirely with eccentric wefts. Weave section three and end its butterfly.

Now begin weaving section four in the same manner as the previous sections. However, when the shape has been woven to the point where the angle of line D becomes very steep, complete the shape by weaving straight rows, shifting the relays as indicated by the dots. Beginning to weave straight rows at this point also prepares the top edge of the example for a horizontal finish.

Weave section five, beginning at its lowest point and filling in along the sides of the previously woven areas. Meet the sides of steep edges row by row, and weave eccentric wefts along low angles. Finish weaving section five with a horizontal row of weaving at the same level as the last horizontal row over section four. Pull the loom beater forward to check the line. Section five must be absolutely level with section four, because the next example should begin with a perfectly straight woven line.

Art is not a handicraft; it is the transmission of feeling the artist has experienced.

—*Leo Tolstoy*

Tips & Advice

The value of cartoons. In addition to providing further experience with eccentric wefts, this example also involves a tapestry cartoon. Drawing images on paper is quite different from weaving those same images. Tapestry weavers need to completely understand both processes and their relationship to each other. Although flexibility and spontaneity are valuable attributes, working within the limits of a predetermined design ensures that the tapestry is proceeding according to the original concept. This degree of control becomes especially reassuring as large portions of a tapestry disappear from sight around the front beam.

Cartoons vs. tapestries. Compare the cartoon with the woven example. The cartoon consists of several contour lines, each drawn with a single, fluid stroke of a pen; the tapestry was created by meticulously constructing shapes within those contours. While the former is a necessary guide to the latter, they differ in several important ways. Most obvious is the quality of the lines between the shapes. While a woven contour line created with eccentric wefts most closely resembles a line drawn with a pen, this technique can only be applied to describe a curved line if its angle is less than 45°. Otherwise, you must construct a stepped edge between adjacent color areas. By experimenting with weaving various shapes, contours, and angles, you can quickly develop an affinity for tapestry technique and eventually prepare designs that maximize the potential of the medium.

Fidelity of tapestry to cartoon. The degree to which the completed tapestry remains truthful to the cartoon depends on several factors:

1. How accurately the contour lines were traced onto the warps. Adjustments may need to be made as you proceed through a design. Compare the measurements of the woven areas with those on the cartoon.

2. Your judgment when shifting a color from one warp to the next. The dots on the warps guide the placement of color in general, but learn to trust your eye; what matters is the visual effect you ultimately wish to achieve.

119

3. Horizontal and vertical shrinkage. Plan for these inevitabilities as you prepare the cartoon. Measure everything you weave, before and after blocking, and keep accurate records.

4. Personal beating style. To accurately evaluate the results of your beating style, take a vertical measurement of a woven area at least 2″ below the fell. Woven rows continue to compress even as they recede from the direct action of the beater.

Weaving adjacent areas. To correctly weave an area adjacent to one that is already woven, consider the directions of the wefts. Look closely at the previously woven area—specifically its first weft turn—and enter the next butterfly to correspond correctly. Then, as the second area meets the first, row by row, all weft turns should occur just as they would have if the two sections had been woven simultaneously.

Personal style. Observe the contrast between the textured blended weft colors and the smooth solid weft colors. These contrasts are emphasized in the example by the close proximity of the two different types of wefts. Leaf through the pages of the book; look at the tapestries with a different eye. This time, look for areas of blended wefts. Compare the effects of these wefts with those of solid-color wefts. Are you beginning to develop preferences? As you observe and experiment further, these preferences will become stronger and eventually contribute to your personal style.

Quality Control Checklist for Tapestries

I'd rather risk an ugly surprise than rely on things I know I can do.

—Helen Frankenthaler

Be your own technical critic. Use this checklist to evaluate your sampler and eventually your tapestries.

1. Scrutinize the woven surface. Every warp should be completely covered, and there should be no weft floats.
2. Loops or tufts on the surface of the tapestry may be caused by either loose weft turns or an excess of weft in the shed. As each weft turn is executed, carry the weft neatly and firmly around the warp. Perfect your bubbling technique; pack only the amount of weft into each shed which comfortably covers the warps.
3. Selvedges should be straight and even. With the weaving of each tapestry or experiment, strive to move toward this standard of excellence.
4. As you weave a tapestry, periodically release the tension on your loom. In this relaxed state, the surface of the tapestry should not pucker excessively. Measure from selvedge to selvedge, and check the measurement against your planned width. Look for drawn-in areas or selvedge bulges. Unweave a bit if necessary. Check vertical measurements while the tapestry is in this state.
5. Put a slight tension on the warps. If the weft has been evenly packed, the warps should be parallel and equally spaced.

Carol K. Russell, Red Column—Crete. Fisk-garn/mattvarp warp, wool and silk weft; 20″ x 28″ (50 by 70 cm.); 1988. Photo: George Mauro. Eccentric wefts, slits, lazy lines, diagonals, blended wefts.

Bottom left: Rojane Lamego, Tecelagem XI. Jute warp; jute, dyed jute, cotton and synthetic weft; 26½″ x 31″ (66 by 77 cm.); 1984. Photo: Wendy Shaull.

Below: Rojane Lamego, Tecelagem VII. Jute warp; jute, dyed jute, cotton, and synthetic weft; 26″ x 17″ (65 by 43 cm.); 1981. Photo: Wendy Shaull.

ECCENTRIC WEFTS

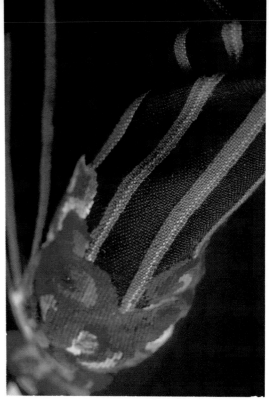

Patricia White, Mime aux Fleurs. *Coat with tapestry inlay, double weave pick-up; 1981.*

Julia Mitchell, Front Garden. *Linen warp, wool weft; 43″ x 61″ (108 by 153 cm.); 1985. Photo: Bruno Debas. Eccentric wefts.*

*Sharon Warren, Water Lilies.
Wool warp and weft; two
panels, each 24″ x 36″ (60 by
90 cm.); 1988. Photo: David
Herberg. Eccentric wefts on lily
pads of panel two.*

Water Lilies (*detail*).

Helga Berry, Glimpse Behind the Moon. Wool warp, wool and silk weft; 63″ x 90″ (158 by 225 cm.); 1986. Photo: Chris Arend. Collection of B. P. Exploration.

Helga Berry, Passage Thru Time. Wool warp; wool, silk, and lurex weft; 38″ x 50″ (95 by 125 cm.); 1988. Photo: Chris Arend.

Versatile Nonwoven Techniques

Up to this point, all examples on the sampler have been constructed by weaving weft yarn through a shed, created by lifting alternate warps. In this chapter, you will encounter soumak, twining, and chaining, three adaptable and useful techniques that require no shed—only tensioned warps. These knotted and wrapped wefts are not to be confused with embroidery, which is stitched onto a woven surface. True tapestry can only be created by weaving the structure of the textile and its images simultaneously; stitched ornamentation would be incongruous. And while the nonwoven techniques described in this chapter enrich a woven surface, their basic structure is compatible in weight and character to that of tapestry. Soumak, twining, and chaining can be used alone, combined with tapestry, or combined with each other, in each case becoming an integral part of the textile.

To fully understand nonwoven techniques, one must consider both of their important functions. First of all, their interesting textures and patterns are valuable additions to a tapestry weaver's visual vocabulary. Less obvious, but no less valuable, are their strictly pragmatic applications. In ancient times, weavers used looms with no reed and yet wove textiles that compare favorably in quality with those from our complicated modern looms. Judging from these textiles, early weavers recognized that the quality of woven cloth is utterly dependent upon the orderliness of the warp—and they spaced that warp, in many cases, with the techniques described in this chapter. Functional rows of twining, soumak, and chaining frequently remained in place after the weaving was completed, providing us with valuable records of their applications.

Other intriguing resources for the study of nonwoven techniques are the folk-art textiles from cultures throughout the world. Knotting, twining, and chaining can be combined with tapestry or other types of plain weave on simple, even portable looms, and skilled weaver/artisans have lavishly embellished almost every type of textile, even those intended for everyday use—from intricately patterned Caucasian rugs, executed entirely with soumak knots, to boldly symbolic Chilkat blankets, worked completely in twining.

Hand-weavers from all cultures are connected by their appreciation for the profound integrity of textiles constructed concurrently with their patterns or designs.

Basic Soumak Technique

General Directions

Choose two colors of weft yarn: a dark value of any hue and a lighter contrasting color. The darker yarn will be used to weave a solid-color tapestry background, and the lighter will be used to emphasize the individual characteristics of each type of soumak knot. Make a butterfly with each of these weft yarns.

A. *A row of open 2/1 soumak.*

B. *A row of closed 2/1 soumak.*

Enter the darker butterfly and weave about ½″ (1.25 cm.) of solid-color background. End this butterfly at either selvedge. The first example will be worked on a closed shed, from the left selvedge to the right. After consulting photograph A for the correct procedure, knot one complete row, creating each knot by carrying the weft from left to right over four warps, then from right to left under two warps. With the usual method for entering a new weft, secure the weft tail at the left around the selvedge warp. You have created a row of open 4/2 soumak. (For an explanation of soumak terminology, see "Tips & Advice.")

To create an identical row of soumak above the first, return the butterfly to the left selvedge. Open the shed opposite the last row of background, and weave the butterfly from the right selvedge to the left. Knot another complete row of soumak; again return the butterfly to the left selvedge, and knot a third row of soumak. End the lighter butterfly. Observe the three densely packed rows of knots and the identical angles of each knot.

Reenter the darker weft, weave about ½″ of background, and end the butterfly. The next example will be a combination of open and closed 2/1 soumak knots. Open the next shed, enter the lighter weft at the right selvedge, and weave one pick, positioning the butterfly at the left selvedge. As before, the soumak knots will be worked on a closed shed. To produce an open 2/1 soumak knot, carry the weft from left to right over two warps, then from right to left under one warp. This change of proportion results in a finer, firmer texture. But because it was worked in the same direction, using the same style of knot, the direction of the slant is the same as the previous example.

After you have completed one row of open 2/1 soumak, knot a row of closed 2/1 soumak, beginning at the right selvedge. The knots of this row will be slanted in the same direction as those in the first row. Consult photograph B for the correct procedure. Next, knot two additional rows of 2/1 soumak, for a total of four. The knots worked from the left selvedge to the right should be the open style (photo A). The knots worked from the right selvedge to the left should be the closed style (photo B). Note that the angles of the knots are consistent in all four rows. To ensure the same slant in successive rows without returning the weft to the opposite selvedge, switch to the other technique as you switch direction. Finish the example with a single pick of plain weave.

Using the darker butterfly, again weave ½″ of solid-color background. Switch to the lighter butterfly, and begin knotting at the left selvedge. The next example of soumak requires eight rows of knots: two rows of open 4/2 soumak, two rows of open 2/1 soumak, two rows of closed 4/2 soumak, and two rows of closed 2/1 soumak. Begin knotting each row at the selvedge where the previous row ended. Do not separate the rows of soumak with plain weave rows. Study the alternating diagonal directions of each row of knots and the resulting knitlike pattern of the soumak. Working the same style of soumak from both directions in two consecutive rows creates a dense surface of opposite-facing diagonal knots.

If you wish, experiment further with soumak. Play with other proportions. Construct isolated areas of soumak over a plain weave background. Try working from the reverse side of the tapestry by knotting from underneath the warps; this is not difficult on a narrow warp, and you will see a very different result. Consult the photographs for guidance and inspiration. Finish the example with ½″ of solid-color background.

Tips & Advice

Terminology. Soumak proportions are referred to by two numbers separated by a slash. The first figure refers to the number of warps over which the weft is carried. The second figure refers to the number of warps under which the weft is carried. For instance, to knot a 4/2 soumak, carry the weft in one direction over four warps and in the opposite direction under two. Some commonly used proportions are·2/1, 4/2, 3/2, 6/3, and 9/3. Of course, within each of these proportions are unlimited possibilities, determined by the choice of weft material and the sett.

"Open" or "closed" soumak refers only to the manner of executing the knots. With open soumak, the working end of the weft is carried over the completed knot to its next position. With closed soumak, the working end of the weft is carried through the loop of the knot, locking each step securely.

Styles of soumak. The instructions for weaving this example are for the classic Oriental method of knotting soumak. Because the Oriental style yields a fine, evenly constructed texture that correlates with, but does not dominate, the flat, regular surface of plain weave, it is the most appropriate soumak for inclusion in a tapestry. Other soumaks result in heavier surfaces with more texture: Greek soumak (three consecutive knots over one warp), Cavandoli knots (two consecutive knots over one warp), or two-color double soumak. While the bulkier soumaks are fascinating to study and experiment with, they may not always combine successfully with delicate tapestry techniques.

Selvedges. At the beginning of each row of soumak and each row of plain weave, carry the weft completely around the selvedge warp.

At the end of each row of soumak, one or two unknotted warps will always remain. As the weft is carried around the selvedge, it should also be carried over this unknotted area, creating visual continuity across the entire row.

Tension. The uniformity of a series of soumak knots is controlled by the degree of tension applied as each individual knot is executed. Yanking the weft very tightly around the warp results in the smallest possible knot. A loosely wrapped warp results in a larger knot. Between these extremes is a moderate degree of tension, resulting in optimum evenness of surface texture and a knot that can be comfortably repeated. Open soumak knots can be most effectively regulated by wrapping the warp(s) with one hand while securing the tension of the previous knot with the other. Closed soumak is the easier of the two techniques to regulate. One hand can separate and lift the warp(s) being wrapped while the other executes the knot. The knotting procedure itself locks the tension. In either case, the tension of each individual soumak knot must be resolved before proceeding with the next one.

With plain weave. For many purposes, rows of plain weave can be woven between rows of soumak. A single row of plain weave is hardly noticeable, functioning only to slightly separate the rows of soumak, or to correctly position the weft for a particular style of knot. Two or more plain weave rows can be woven between each row of soumak to create a very different textile structure, one that is predominantly plain weave. This sturdy textile can support areas of widely distributed, loosely executed soumak—areas intended only as decorative or textural patterns.

Each row of plain weave should be woven through the shed opposite the previous row of plain weave.

Talent develops in quiet places, character in the full current of human life.

—Johann Wolfgang von Goethe

Beating. Complete rows of soumak, with or without intervening rows of tabby, benefit greatly by being packed firmly with the loom beater. Part of the beauty and technical desirability of knotted techniques is their density and weight. Of course, independent or eccentric areas of soumak must be beaten with a hand beater.

How much weft you will need. Soumak requires more weft yarn than plain weave to cover the same distance. It could be two or three times as much, but the exact amount depends upon the soumak proportions (4/2, 6/3, etc.) and the tension of each stitch. To determine exactly how much yarn would be required to knot a given soumak proportion across a given distance, knot a 2″ width with the intended weft yarn. Remove the knots and measure the yarn. Knowing how much yarn is required to knot 2″ will give you the correct factor for determining how much yarn would be needed to cover any distance.

Consistent diagonals. There are two methods of repeating the diagonal direction of successive rows of soumak knots. The first method requires returning the weft to the opposite selvedge at the beginning of each row and repeating the soumak style (either open or closed) of the previous row. In other words, to create a series of soumak rows with identical diagonals, work each row in the same style and from the same direction. The second method may be worked from either direction, but requires switching between the two styles of knots. In other words, to create consistent diagonals in successive rows of soumak knotted from opposite directions, switch to the opposite style of knot as you switch direction.

Twist. As the weft is pulled from the butterfly and wrapped around the warps, it tends to either untwist or twist more tightly. Any change in the character of the weft yarn will appear on the knotted surface; a kinky weft cannot be knotted evenly. A more serious problem is that single-spun yarns will unspin and thus weaken. Pause periodically and spin the weft between your fingers to return the yarn to its normal twist.

Choosing materials. Knotting an area of soumak with weft yarns differing in characteristics from those of its surrounding area could introduce exciting contrasts of texture, color, or luster. For instance, consider inserting soumak knots worked with a smooth, lustrous rayon weft to contrast with the light-absorbent wool surface of the tapestry weave. Or to delicately emphasize the edge of a leaf or flower, knot a row of soumak using a pearly silk weft. To create slender, unobtrusive soumak outlines, I frequently use a very fine single-spun wool weft. Oversized soumak knots worked with handspun, unspun, or other heavy wefts are best reserved for rugs or other textiles. Traditional tapestry, with its even, flat-woven surface, could easily become overwhelmed by large-scale soumak knots.

Reversible effects. Using a mirror, examine the reverse side of the soumak examples. Notice that there are no diagonals, that the knotted surface resembles evenly stitched needlepoint, and that the surface of the soumak is not raised above that of the plain weave. Understanding that soumak is not reversible may affect your choice of technique, especially for outlining. Soumak executed on the reverse side of a tapestry appears very different when viewed from the front. And although either effect is entirely acceptable, a weaver/designer usually prefers one or the other.

It is art that MAKES life, makes interest, makes importance, for our consideration and application of these things, and I know of no substitute whatever for the force and beauty of its process.

—Henry James

128

Weft Twining and Chaining

General Directions

Choose contrasting weft yarns: a light value of any hue for weaving the background, and one or more darker hues for the twining and chaining. Make a butterfly with only the lighter yarn, and enter it into the next shed. Weave about ½″ of background, and end the butterfly in either shed.

Cut a single 80″ (200 cm.) length of the darker yarn, double it, carry the center loop under and around the warp at the left selvedge, and draw both tails through the loop. You have thus attached the weft to the selvedge warp with a single ring hitch—a most useful weaver's knot. The first example will be twined with the two 40″ (100 cm.) lengths of weft, each of which is approximately half the usual weight of weft.

Working from left to right on a closed shed, carry one of the wefts under the second warp from the selvedge, then carry the other weft under the third warp from the selvedge. Continue in this manner, carrying the wefts alternately under each warp. Observe that the wefts cross in the spaces between the warps. At the right selvedge, cross the wefts and continue twining in the opposite direction.

After two complete rows have been twined, there will be two weft tails at the left selvedge. Open a weaving shed and secure these tails in the usual invisible manner.

Weave another ½″ of background and end the butterfly. The next example of twining involves longer floats between interlacings, worked with a heavier weft. Using the single ring hitch, secure an 80″ length of double-weight weft around the warp at the left selvedge. Twine two complete rows, carrying each pair of wefts alternately under two consecutive warps. Observe the heavier texture of this example of twining, as compared with that of the previous example.

Weave another ½″ of background and end the butterfly. An example of two-color twining will be created next. This time cut a 40″ length of each of two highly contrasting colors of weft yarns. Knot the ends of both lengths around the selvedge warp at the left, leaving tails of at least 4″ (10 cm.). As in the first example of twining, carry the wefts alternately under each warp across the row. Unknot the weft tails at the left selvedge and secure them as follows: Open a shed. Observe that one of the two weft colors is consistently lowered with this set of warps. Secure the weft tail of that color over the lowered warps in the usual manner. Change sheds and secure the other weft tail over the lowered warps in that shed. Observe that the weft tails have been secured invisibly, preserving the strong pattern of the two-color weft twining.

At the right selvedge, twist the two wefts for the return trip. The twining of the next row should result in a series of chevrons—opposite-facing diagonals of two contrasting colors. To achieve this effect precisely, observe which color is traveling over each warp in the first row, and carry the same color over that warp in the second row.

Weave another ½″ of background and end the butterfly. Next, twine a single row of two-color twining, interlacing around adjacent pairs of warps with doubled wefts. As only a single row is twined, the effect is quite different from that of the previous example. Two rows of two-color twining create an emphatic pattern of opposite-facing diagonals, while one row creates a spiral. Secure the weft tails at both selvedges and again weave ½″ of background.

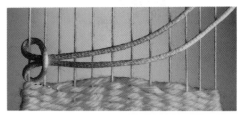

A single-ring hitch, used to secure the weft to the selvedge warp at the beginning of a row of weft twining.

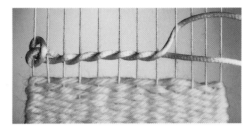

The twining procedure.

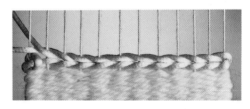

Two complete rows of twining.

Twining, using double the weight of weft and surrounding two warps at a time.

Twining with two strands each of two weft colors.

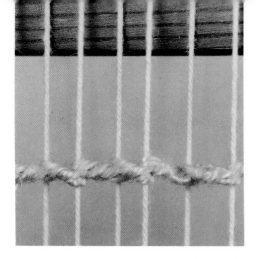

A row of chaining installed across the top of a tapestry loom with no reed. The chained loops retain the sett as the warp is advanced. Photographed by George Goodwin.

The beginning of the chaining procedure.

The first chained loop.

Next, create a single row of weft chaining. Most admired as a textural accent or wide outline, chaining is also quite useful for controlling the sett while beaming or advancing a warp, since many vertical tapestry looms have warp and cloth beams but no reed. A row of chaining installed across the warp functions in much the same manner as a reed. The chained stitches surround each warp, providing a precisely regulated series of slots through which the warp can be wound.

Looped in a continuous series around each warp, weft chaining is theoretically similar to the single crochet stitch. To create a single row of chaining on your sampler, cut a 90″ (225 cm.) length of weft yarn, and tie one end of it to the warp at the left selvedge, leaving a tail long enough to be secured invisibly. Make a loop with the yarn and close its open end by twist-ing it slightly. Draw another loop from the working end of the yarn through the original loop. Observe that by pulling on the working end of the yarn, you can tighten the original loop to form a knot and adjust the size of the new loop. Adjust the new loop to about 4″ in diameter. At this point, the first of the series of adjustable chain stitches has been installed onto the warp.

Reaching through the loop with your right hand, lift the warp at the left selvedge. With your left hand, feed another loop from the working end of the weft under the warp and through the loop in your right hand. Adjust the chain stitch around the first warp by pulling on the working end of the weft. Again reach through the loop with your right hand, lift the next warp in sequence, chain around it, and adjust. Repeat the chaining procedure around each warp. At the right selvedge, lock the chain to keep it from unraveling; draw the working end of the weft completely through the last loop. The chain stitches should be regular in size, corresponding exactly to the sett: six to the inch. Secure the weft tails at both selvedges in the usual manner, and finish the example with ½″ of background.

Locking the chain at the opposite end of the row.

Tips & Advice

Twining vs. tapestry weave. Observe the examples of twining. Each warp or group of warps has a weft traveling over it and a weft traveling under it. In this manner, twining is similar to tapestry weave, although the twisting action of the wefts between the warps is different. It is this twisting action that directly affects the character of contrasting lines created with twining. Two picks of tapestry weave have a pronounced wavy appearance. A single row of twining—more or less equivalent in weight and action to these two picks—is much less wavy. For this reason, twining may be used to describe very smooth, fluid outlines for either geometric or eccentric shapes.

Establishing the sett. The twisting action of the two wefts also provides the requisite firmness to each twined row if the technique is used for establishing the sett. If a tapestry loom has no reed (and there are many such looms in existence), or if a small tapestry is being woven on a frame loom, the warps must be regularly spaced before the weaving can proceed. On a loom with both cloth and warp beams, the warp is tied in bights onto the front apron bar. On a frame loom, the warp is wound around a series of nails or around the frame itself. With either type of loom, one or two rows of twining are required to space the warp evenly. This type of twining should be done with a sturdy cord. Plied linen and cotton are both good choices. The weight of the yarn should be chosen according to the desired sett: For a close sett, twine with a fine yarn. For a widely spaced warp, use a heavier yarn.

Twine from selvedge to selvedge until the warps are evenly spaced. Secure the weft tails in the usual manner, or braid them at the selvedge if this detail is appropriate for the type of textile being woven. If the twining is strictly functional and will be removed later, simply knot the weft tails temporarily at one selvedge. Above the rows of twining, weave a heading as usual.

Native Americans. Navajo weavers twine at both ends and along both sides of their beautiful rugs, to secure the sett of their meticulous continuous warps and to reinforce all four unfringed selvedges. At the completion of the weaving, the tails of the twinings are braided.

Warp control. Because twining and chaining contribute to the structure of a weft-face textile, they are interchangeable as nonwoven accents or outlines. However, choosing between the techniques for warp control requires more judgment. As discussed previously, twining is a useful device for spacing the warps at the beginning of the weaving, while chaining is the better choice for controlling the sett of a continuous warp. A row of chaining may be temporarily installed across the entire width of the loom, allowing the warp to be wound through its accurately spaced stitches.

Observe the row of chaining installed below the top crossbar of the tapestry loom in the photograph. The warp, which happened to be five yards long in this case, was first divided into sections 2″ (5 cm.) wide, then beamed through the pegged raddle at the top of the loom. After being tied in 1″ bights to the front apron bar and tensioned, the warp was advanced slightly to move the knots around the bottom beam. With the warps stretched between the top and bottom beams, the initial spacing procedure, which must be done by hand, warp by warp, proceeded efficiently.

The learning process follows the creative one. After the heat and excitement of production comes a period of cool assessment from which much can be learned. Points arise in the mind which start a train of thought. . . .

—Theo Moorman

Then, directly below the top beam, a row of chaining was installed, corresponding to the sett of the perfectly spaced warp. To keep the chain from winding forward or backward with the warp, it was tied by its two long tails to the top corners of the loom. With the chained "reed" tied securely, the entire warp could be rolled through its accurate slots onto the cloth beam. At this point, the warp was unwound from the cloth beam, untied, and with the usual degree of hand-held tension, wound once more through the chain. The second beaming procedure ensured that the entire five-yard warp could be advanced as needed with perfect tension and sett, the two factors most crucial to a tapestry warp, and sufficient justification for knotting the warp to the front apron bar a second time.

Tools. To facilitate the chaining procedure, use a crochet hook to draw each new loop through the previous loop.

Experimenting. The possibilities for experimentation with weft twining and chaining are almost endless. Try using contrasting hues and values in various combinations. Twine with two weft yarns of different weights. Also try varying the lengths of the interlacings.

A Chilkat dancing blanket from the Tlingit tribe of the Pacific Northwest. Tapestry twined in both warp and weft directions. Warp of goat and cedar bark, weft of goat and sheep. Collection of the Textile Museum, Washington, D.C.

Lightweight soumak hanging. Hand-spun wool warp, single-spun wool weft; 94″ x 24″ (235 by 60 cm.). Photo: George Mauro. Collection of Jason Nazmiyal/Rug & Kilim. Two-color weft twining, offset pick-and-pick.

Turkish rug worked completely in soumak. Collection of Carol K. Russell.

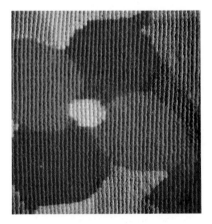
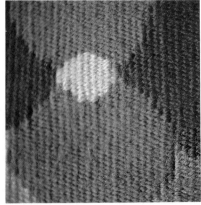

Same design in Swedish knots (upside down soumak) and regular tapestry. Photo: Carmelina Margaret D'Amelio. Collection of Mary D'Amelio.

VERSATILE NONWOVEN TECHNIQUES

Horse cover from Iran. Fine, soft, two-ply wool warp; very fine single-spun wool weft; 51" x 45" (128 by 113 cm.). Photo: George Mauro. Collection of Jason Nazmiyal/Rug & Kilim. Soumak borders and soumak outlining of every angle.

Russian soumak. Two-ply wool warp, single-spun wool weft; 28½" x 22" (71 by 55 cm.). Photo: George Mauro. Collection of Jason Nazmiyal/Rug & Kilim. Soumak as dominant design element over plain weave background.

VERSATILE NONWOVEN TECHNIQUES

Outlining Techniques

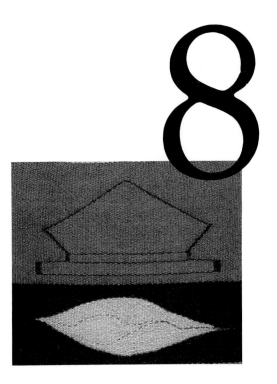

While it is not necessary to outline woven shapes, the technique may prove useful in certain instances. For example, if a background in a tapestry design does not contrast sufficiently in hue or value with the positive shapes, outlining those shapes with a contrasting color would define their contours and separate them from the too-similar background. Or, to develop a unifying rhythm, emphasize the similarity of a series of curved contours with echoes of very fine eccentric outlines. In the Chilkat Dancing Blanket, the energetic spirit of the geometric, totemlike design is intensified by its highly contrasting outlines.

As with other tapestry images, woven outlines must be planned for and integrated into the textile in coordination with their adjacent areas. This need for prior orchestration is the consistent underlying difference between tapestry and other art forms. Painted, drawn, or stitched outlines are usually added to contours—contours developed independently of the background. Outlining in these mediums can be either planned meticulously or added spontaneously. In both cases, the artist simply applies the chosen color, adding appropriate emphasis or enhancement to an existing contour. With tapestry outlines, spontaneity of execution is inhibited; but spontaneity of effect is quite possible with a bit of careful planning on the part of the weaver/designer.

To expand your outlining possibilities, consider the techniques sampled in the previous chapter. Woven and nonwoven techniques can both be applied as outlines, depending upon the circumstances involved and the personal preferences of the weaver/designer.

Outlining Curved Contours

General Directions

Weave this example according to the leaf design on the next page. It is not necessary to trace an exact cartoon; the shape may be interpreted freely during the weaving process by developing curved lines with angles similar to those in the design.

Choose a color of weft yarn for weaving the background. It should be of a medium value. Make two butterflies with this weft yarn. The weft yarn for weaving the leaf should be a very light value blend of two or more closely related hues. Make one butterfly with this yarn. Choose a color of weft yarn for weaving the outlines. It should be of a very dark value. Make one butterfly with this weft yarn.

Into the next weaving shed, enter the two background butterflies traveling in opposite directions. Weave about 1″ (2.5 cm.) of background, then rest the butterflies at the selvedges.

Next, weaving independently with the background butterfly at the left, develop the moderately steep angle of curved line A, ending at point D. Then, weaving independently with the background butterfly at the right, develop the gentle slope of curved line B, ending at point C. Because point D is higher than point C, more rows will be woven at the left than at the right. Rest both background butterflies at the selvedges.

Enter the outlining weft color at point E. Weave it to point D and back again to point E, where the butterfly will rest. Enter the lightest butterfly at point D, and with it weave a continuous curved pick to point C. Entering the leaf weft across its entire width enables it to travel correctly in both directions. Next, develop the curved shape below the lower vein between points H and C by weaving rows of eccentric wefts with the lightest butterfly. Then, to avoid trapping this weft under the vein, weave it to point D, where it will rest.

With the outlining butterfly, weave a single pick from point C to point H, and drop it to the back of the tapestry. With the lightest butterfly, weave the next curved shape over the lower vein, between points G and F. Again rest this butterfly near point D.

Carry the outlining butterfly to the front of the tapestry at point G, and with it weave a single row over the second curved shape. Again rest the outlining butterfly at point C. With the lightest butterfly, develop the curved contour across the top of the leaf. End this butterfly.

Weave two rows with the outlining butterfly between points C and D. End the outlining butterfly. Fill in the areas along both sides of the leaf, weaving with one background butterfly at a time. Then continue weaving straight rows, relaying both butterflies randomly, until 1″ of background has been woven over the leaf. End both background butterflies.

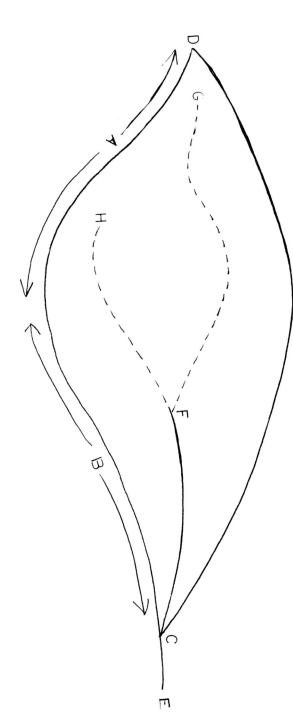

Cartoon for outlining curved contours.

Tips & Advice

Critical points. To create a smooth, uninterrupted outline and to sharply define the graceful shape of the leaf, avoid carrying the lightest weft too far at points C and D. It is at these two crucial points that the upper and lower outlines meet, and it is here that their continuity must not be broken with an invasion of contrasting weft.

Eccentric wefts. An appropriate final touch to an area of eccentric wefts would be to continue weaving with the same weft, surrounding the upper curve of the shape with one or two continuous picks. These smooth, curved rows soften the effect of a stepped angle, clarify and emphasize the curved contour, and in some instances coordinate the following shed for weaving a contrasting outline.

Uncoordinated sheds. During the weaving of this example, it may be necessary to adjust an uncoordinated shed. Remember that if a weaving shed has one or more uncoordinated areas, switch to the previous shed and lay a length of weft yarn across each uncoordinated area. Then, switch back to the weaving shed, which should now be correct.

Short outlines. With a similar technique, short outlines (dotted or solid) can be easily inserted over a curved contour by laying in lengths of contrasting weft.

Emphasis. Observe the difference in emphasis between the subtle, lightly dotted outlines and the solid, two-pick outlines.

Graded outlines. Consider the possibility of varying the width of a certain crucial outline in a tapestry design. Create a graded one. At one end of the line, weave a heavy outline (four or five rows). Then reduce it gradually to a gentle whisper of a few carefully positioned dots.

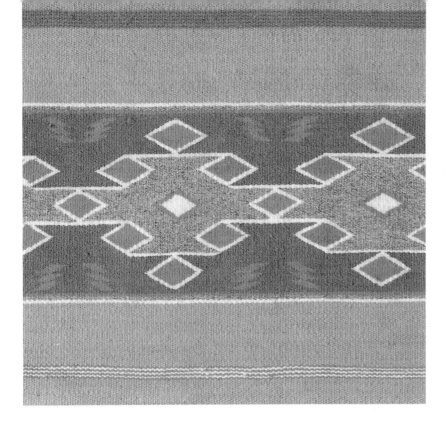

Navajo Rug, Crystal Pattern (detail). Cotton warp, single-spun wool weft; 29" x 39" (73 by 98 cm.). Photo: George Mauro. Collection of Carol and Ken Hopper. Fifty-fifty wavy stripes, outlined diamonds.

Turkish Salt Bag (detail). Two-ply wool warp, fine single-spun wool weft; 43" x 34" (108 by 85 cm.). Photo: George Mauro. Collection of Jason Nazmiyal/Rug & Kilim. Outlining, 50-50 wavy stripes, diagonals.

OUTLINING TECHNIQUES

Jan Yoors, Captives. Woven by
Annabert and Marianne Yoors.
Cotton warp, wool weft. 8' x 7'
(2.4 by 2.1 m.); 1956. Photo:
George Cserna.

OUTLINING TECHNIQUES

Tricia Goldberg, Gesture. Cotton, wool, and silk materials; 8″ x 8″ (20 by 20 cm.); 1988. Photo: Bruce Handelsman.

Trudi Eldridge, Orchids and My Imagination. *Wool warp and weft; 40″ x 30″ (100 by 75 cm.); 1986.*

Victor Jacoby, Tropical Memories. *Cotton warp, wool weft; 23½″ x 53½″ (58 by 134 cm.); 1988. Photo: James D. Toms.*

Contrast. Contrasts of value, hue, and intensity play an important part of outline design. This example illustrates strong contrasts between all three weft colors, creating the most emphatic outlines. Subtle outlines are created with less contrast between the figure and its outline, and/or between the outline and the adjacent background.

Texture. Observe the difference in visual texture between the background area woven in straight, orderly rows with a solid-color weft, and the leaf woven at eccentric angles with blended wefts.

Fine yarns. It is possible to delicately outline a curved contour with a very fine weft, one much finer than the one used to weave the main design. A few isolated rows, inserted with a different weft, would not significantly compromise the structure of the textile.

Outlining Geometric Shapes

General Directions

This example should be woven according to the geometric design in the illustration—a design planned to provide experience with those circumstances encountered outlining simple shapes. As in the previous section, do not trace the lines onto the warps. Interpret the design freely, developing similar angles and shapes of any desired size. The execution of this example involves tapestry skills previously acquired by weaving the rest of the sampler. These skills, and their refinement, are valuable tools, applied to either geometric, representational, or abstract tapestry designs.

Choose a color of weft yarn for weaving the background, with a value from the middle range. Make two butterflies. Choose a color of weft yarn for the geometric shapes, with a value from the very lightest range. Make two butterflies with this yarn. Choose a color of weft yarn for the outlining— very dark or very intense, to contrast sharply with both the background and the geometric shapes. Make two butterflies with the outlining weft.

Into the next shed, enter the two background butterflies traveling in opposite directions. Relaying the wefts randomly, weave about 1″ of background. Rest both butterflies at the selvedges.

Begin the development of the first rectangular shape by constructing its lower horizontal outline. First, enter one of the darkest butterflies around a lowered warp 2″ (5 cm.) from the right selvedge. Then enter the other darkest butterfly around a lowered warp 2″ from the left selvedge. Weave the butterflies toward each other, meeting at any point. Change sheds, reverse the directions of the butterflies, and weave them back to the positions at which they were entered. These two picks outline the bottom of the first rectangular shape and define its width. And, at this point, both outlining butterflies are correctly positioned for weaving the vertical outlines at the sides of the rectangle.

The rectangle should be woven next. Into the next shed, directly above the outline, enter one of the lightest butterflies at the right edge of the rectangle. Avoid entering or weaving the lightest weft around the two warps at the extreme right of the rectangle. These two warps and the two warps at the extreme left of the rectangle will be covered by the darkest weft as it outlines, vertically, the rectangle's sides. With the lightest butterfly, weave

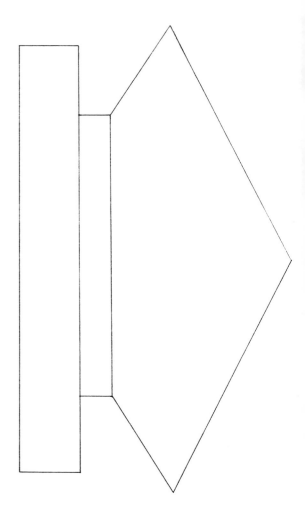

To weave this geometric design, rotate it 90 degrees to the left.

141

the rectangle to a height of about 1″. End the weaving of this area at the right edge of the rectangle by dropping the lightest butterfly temporarily to the back of the tapestry. Beat the rows of the rectangle, and every incomplete row thereafter, with a hand beater.

Next, weave the vertical outlines at the sides of the rectangle. With one outlining butterfly at a time, weave back and forth over two warps. Build the vertical outlines to the top of the rectangle. Observe the slits at the sides of both outlines. When the vertical outlines are complete, weave the two darkest butterflies toward each other, meeting at any point over the top of the rectangle. Change sheds, reverse the directions of the outlining wefts, and return them to the sides of the rectangle, where they should be dropped temporarily to the back of the tapestry. You have now outlined four sides of the rectangle. Compare the narrow, two-pick, horizontal outlines with the wider, vertical outlines executed over two warps. Fill in the background areas at both sides until the entire weaving row is level again.

To construct a smaller rectangle directly above the first, open the next weaving shed and carry the lightest butterfly to the front of the tapestry. It should enter the shed at a point about 1″ from the right edge of the first rectangle and travel to a point about 1″ from its left edge. Having defined the width of the second rectangle, build a second rectangle about ½″ (1.25 cm.) high. End the weaving of this rectangle at its right edge by dropping the lightest butterfly to the back of the tapestry.

Carry both outlining butterflies to the front of the tapestry at the bottom edges of the second rectangle. To create the narrowest possible vertical outlines, wrap the two warps adjacent to the rectangle with outlining weft (an easier procedure if you raise the warps being wrapped). Observe the very fine, if somewhat unstable, outlines. When both warps have been wrapped, the outlines may be anchored by weaving a two-pick horizontal outline over the top of the second rectangle. Rest the outlining butterflies at the upper corners of the rectangle.

Fill in the background to the top of the second rectangle. Then, with the background butterflies, develop the steep lower angles of the diamond by shifting both background wefts one warp every four rows. At the completion of the lower angles of the diamond, rest the background butterflies at the selvedges.

With the darkest wefts, outline the two steep diagonal lines with rows of closed soumak knots worked around every warp. Observe that the soumak knots securely surround the warps, conforming neatly to the degree of the angle with no excessive floats. Rest the outlining butterflies at the top of the diagonal lines.

The next step is to fill in the area between the diagonal lines with the lightest weft. To execute the diamond symmetrically, you need two butterflies traveling in opposite directions. Therefore, carry the lightest butterfly from the back of the tapestry to the right edge of the second rectangle. Then enter the other lightest butterfly at its opposite edge. Relaying or dovetailing the two butterflies randomly, weave the entire diamond shape. Meet, row by row, the outlined edge of the bottom of the diamond; then develop the angles of its top by shifting the wefts one warp every row. End the butterflies at the top of the diamond by overlapping their tails over the center warp.

Through the next shed, weave both outlining wefts to the top of the diamond and dovetail them around the center warp. Change sheds, reverse the directions of the wefts, and weave a second outlining pick over the first.

The mutual influencing of colors we call—interaction. Seen from the opposite viewpoint, it is—interdependence.

—Josef Albers

End both outlining wefts at the sides of the diamond. Compare the outlines created with eccentric wefts with the soumak outlines. Fill in the background at both sides of the example. Continue weaving another inch of background above the outlined shape.

Completing the example of outlined geometric shapes concludes the weaving of your tapestry sampler. With warp yarn, weave a heading 1″ wide, corresponding to the heading at the beginning of the sampler. Then weave a few rows of fuzzy yarn to secure the heading temporarily. Untie the sampler from your loom and admire your beautiful accomplishments.

This detail of a Greek tapestry, from the collection of the author, illustrates the outlining of geometric shapes. Photographed by George Goodwin.

Tips & Advice

Slits. A narrow vertical outline wrapped around a single warp, and a vertical outline woven over two warps, result in slits between the outline and adjacent areas. Slits and their structural hazards should be considered when planning outlines as part of a tapestry design. If a vertical outline is very short, slits are not a problem. But if slits along an outline are more than 1″ long and the tapestry has been designed to be mounted with the warp horizontal, woven links, weft crossings, or another method of slit control will be necessary.

Direction of wrap. While you are creating the narrowest vertical outline, note that it is possible to wrap a warp from either direction. To decide which direction is correct, first determine into which shed, and from which direction, the outlining weft must be woven to create the next contiguous horizontal outline. If the warp has been wrapped from the correct direction, the outlining weft should be in position to enter the next shed correctly, with no weft float.

Finding the center. The exact center of a tapestry design planned for an even number of warps is a space between two warps; the exact center of a tapestry design planned for an odd number of warps is a warp. Consider these circumstances as you plan the centering of a design and its symmetry.

Dropping back. Outlining wefts may be dropped to the back of the tapestry as they complete a segment of an outline. It is then possible for them to reemerge invisibly in any position to weave the next outline.

Symmetry. Row-by-row symmetry is crucial to the development of precise geometric shapes, with or without outlines. Triangles, diamonds, or any shape expanding or contracting symmetrically, should be developed with wefts traveling in opposite directions. Therefore, symmetrical shapes should be outlined with opposing wefts. It follows that background areas on either side must also be woven with opposing wefts, corresponding correctly to the edges of the shape and its outlines.

On the other hand, simple square or rectangular shapes can be woven with a single weft traveling from one edge of the shape to the other.

Outlining with eccentric wefts. Diagonal contours that are not excessively steep can be successfully outlined with eccentric wefts. But an eccentric outline woven along a steep diagonal contour appears sloppy and unstable relative to the adjacent woven texture. This occurs because steeply pitched wefts cannot interlace with the warps at normal intervals—they span a greater distance traveling from warp to warp, floating dangerously and altering the woven texture. A steep angle is the perfect opportunity to apply one of the nonwoven techniques as outlining.

Reversing the irreversible. After the tapestry sampler is removed from the loom, observe the reverse side of the soumak outlines (and the soumak examples as well). The opposite side of soumak—a finer, less bulky outline—may be preferable to you. If you are able to reach below (on a horizontal loom) or behind (on a vertical loom) a tapestry in progress, soumak can be easily worked in reverse. Or if you prefer weaving tapestries from the reverse side, the opposite soumak texture happens automatically on the right side.

Other outlines. Experiment with other nonwoven methods for outlining, especially along steep angles or around irregular shapes. Chaining works very well. A chained outline is flat and intricately textured, its width determined by the weight of the weft yarn. Weft twining, worked in a fine yarn, results in a narrow, perfectly flat, and smoothly textured outline. Worked in a heavier weft, a twined outline is wider, but not raised above the surface of the weaving in the manner of soumak. And, amazingly, twined outlines, while they conform to any contour, however steep, are straighter and more consistent than woven outlines. Because of their stability in any direction and their contribution to the structure of the textile, all of the nonwoven techniques are worthy of being included as tapestry outlines.

One of my main concerns is that tapestry should look like tapestry and not paint.

—Christine Laffer

144

Blocking, Finishing, and Mounting

W hen cutting or untying a tapestry from the loom, leave warp fringes of at least 10″ (25 cm.). Then allow the tapestry to lie flat on its face for one or two days. A weft-face textile is woven under extreme tension; a period of relaxation restores and stabilizes normal warp/weft relationships. Note that it is possible to gently handle the tapestry with no unraveling of the headings, as they are safely contained within the rows of fuzzy yarn.

With the tapestry at ease and conveniently wrong-side-up, tie and trim the weft tails, to prevent them from migrating to the front of the tapestry and to direct them away from its edges. The knotted wefts and their positions on the back of the tapestry are subsequently set by the blocking process. Ideally, each weft tail should be at least 3″ (7.5 cm.) long, to allow for the tying of a secure overhand knot with a close neighbor, but a square knot can also be used for tying shorter tails.

The reverse side of a tapestry after it has been removed from the loom. Photographed by Parklane Photo Labs.

The reverse side of a tapestry after the warps have been knotted and the weft tails tied. Photographed by Parklane Photo Labs.

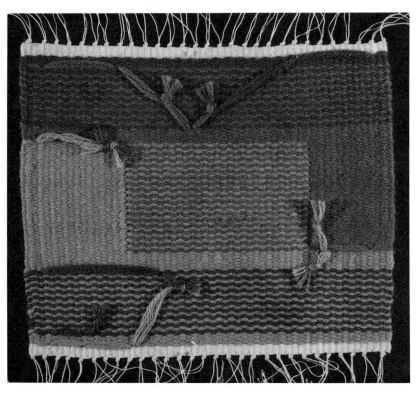

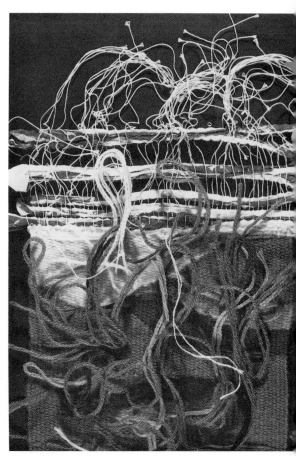

Two weft tails secured at the selvedge according to the author's alternative method and knotted together during finishing. Photographed by George Goodwin.

Using a blunt needle to pull the warps from inside the rows of fuzzy yarn. Photographed by George Goodwin.

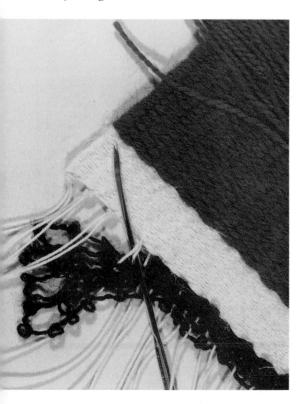

Many weft tails pair up logically—for example, two wefts entered or deleted by overlapping a warp from different directions. These wefts should be knotted together and trimmed above each knot. To keep the edges of the tapestry uncluttered, weft tails near the selvedges or hems should be directed toward, and tied to, those closer to the center of the tapestry. Any remaining slits can be sewn at this time and the tails of the sewing thread secured to each other or to nearby weft tails. The back of a tapestry is seldom as beautiful as its front, but it should be tidy and controlled. Most important, there should be no excess bulk or weight of weft yarn.

Instructions for knotting the warps follow next. Some weavers, however, recommend blocking a tapestry prior to this procedure, to further relax the warps and draw them into their natural relationship with the wefts. Other weavers prefer to knot the warps and establish the edges of a tapestry before permanently setting its surface. Excellent results have been observed in tapestries blocked according to both theories, making a specific recommendation difficult. My advice is to experiment with both procedures on small tapestry samples and establish your personal preference based on the results. To block first, skip to the blocking instructions, leaving the rows of fuzzy yarn in place to contain the heading.

To avoid distorting the edges of the tapestry and to ensure small, unobtrusive knots, tie the warps two at a time. Using a blunt needle, separate and pull the first pair of warps from inside the rows of fuzzy yarn. Then, with an overhand knot, knot the warps tightly at the edge of the heading. Repeat the procedure across one hem, then knot the warps along the other hem. Note that the rows of fuzzy yarn retain the straight line of the heading and prevent the first rows of weft from unweaving during the knotting process. The knotted warps can be trimmed to a length of about ½″ (1.25 cm.).

Blocking a tapestry takes about five days, during which it lies flat on its face, in a damp state. Thus, you will need a floor or surface that will not be harmed by moisture and that will not bleed alien colors into the tapestry. Because nails can be driven into it, a large sheet of plywood works well, especially for tapestries requiring a bit of selvedge adjustment. For tapestries requiring only blocking, not nailing, I have used a tile floor.

First, cover the plywood or other surface with plastic sheeting; inexpensive shower curtain liners work very well. The plastic protects the tapestry as well as the surface. Then, over the plastic, place a layer of damp towels edge to edge (no overlaps or lumps—they would be next to the front surface of the tapestry). White or very light-colored towels are preferable. Even towels that show no visible signs of bleeding during washing may transfer dye if they remain damp over an extended period of time. The towels should be about as wet as if they had come from the spin cycle of a washing machine: They should not drip, and it should not be easy to wring water from them. Place the tapestry face down over the damp towels and cover it with another layer of damp towels.

If any realignment of the selvedges is required, it should be done after the tapestry has been surrounded with damp towels for about 24 hours—in other words, after the tapestry has been slowly and almost completely penetrated with moisture. While the tapestry is in this vulnerable state, certain adjustments are possible, but they must be handled very carefully. Uncover the tapestry. Gently pull out any drawn-in areas of the selvedges. Observe the pliability of the damp tapestry. Carefully nail the newly established edge into place using aluminum or any rustproof tacks. Realign any drawn-out areas of the selvedges and nail them. Spray the adjusted area lightly with water to reinforce the blocking at those points. Again, cover the tapestry with the damp towels.

Steam can be used very judiciously during the blocking process. Warm, moist applications may cause the tapestry to shrink a bit—a potential advantage to a puckered tapestry surface requiring selective shrinking. Steam can also be applied to reinforce the set of any realigned selvedges. Be certain about the fastness of the dyes of the weft yarns before applying steam to a damp tapestry. Yarns that do not bleed when merely damp may bleed under the simultaneous application of heat and moisture. To conclusively test for fastness under extremes of heat and moisture, place scraps of wet, weft yarns between wet, white paper towels. Using a hot iron, thoroughly steam the yarns and the towels. If no dye bleeds onto the towels, the tapestry can be safely steamed. However, to avoid crushing the texture of its surface, always steam a tapestry through a cloth, using a light touch. The objective is to set the weft yarns, not flatten them.

The next part of the blocking procedure has many variables. For instance, in a heated room during the winter, a tapestry can remain covered with towels for three full days with no danger of mildew. Under these circumstances, a greater concern would be to avoid drying a wool tapestry too quickly. Therefore, after three days, remove only the top layer of towels, leaving the lower layer to slow the drying process from below. On the other hand, during a humid summer heat wave, two days would be the maximum time to keep a tapestry moist. At that point, all damp towels should be removed and the tapestry placed directly onto the plastic to air-dry completely. These examples represent the two extremes of blocking conditions. Use good judgment, and consider the temperature and humidity of the room in which the tapestry is being blocked. Theoretically, to be thoroughly blocked, a tapestry must become evenly penetrated with moisture, then allowed to dry very slowly, away from direct heat.

Hemming is another aspect of tapestry finishing about which there are many theories. In general, the headings should be turned back at both edges and invisibly but securely hand-stitched. A favorite method of many weavers is to weave about 1" (2.5 cm.) of solid-color tapestry background above the first heading, then a row of soumak knots marking the actual edge of the tapestry. This highly recommended method, duplicated at both ends of a tapestry, results in perfectly even hems, well-concealed headings, two uniform edges, and the flattest possible folds in a heavy textile.

The hemming and mounting of a tapestry must be considered at the same time. If a tapestry is designed to be mounted by a selvedge, both vertical edges are hemmed in the same manner, and a separate, horizontally installed mounting tape is stitched to the top selvedge. If a

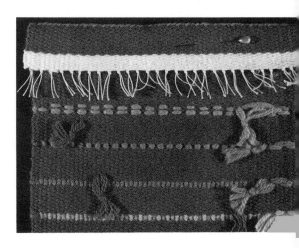

Note the inch of tapestry weave above the white heading, and the row of soumak marking the actual edge. Photographed by Parklane Photo Labs.

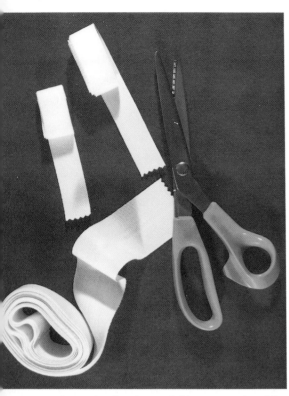

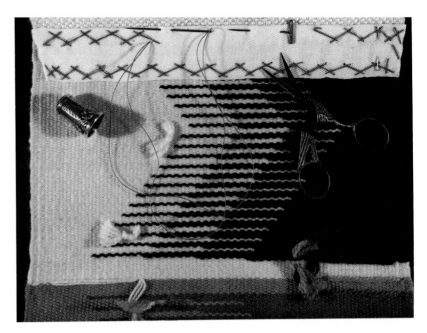

Carpet binding being sewn onto the back of the tapestry.

Carpet binding is available in several widths.

Different widths of Velcro that have been machine-stitched to lengths of carpet binding.

tapestry is designed to be mounted by one of its hems, that edge can be turned back and hemmed with the installation of the mounting tape, with the other edge hemmed in the usual manner.

In either case, the warp knots must be covered. These knots are crucial to the structural integrity of a tapestry, and they should be shielded from abrasion and long-term deterioration. Cotton twill carpet binding (also called "twill tape") stitched over the turned-back edges of a tapestry covers the warp knots and creates neat, strong hems. Because most cotton textile products have been treated with chemical sizings that are potentially erosive to tapestry materials, wash, dry, and press the carpet bindings before stitching them to the tapestry. Carpet binding comes in different widths. For hemming only, not mounting, use a width that covers the warp knots and most of the heading. With the heading of the tapestry folded back, pin the carpet binding in place. The inside edge should cover the short warp fringes. The outside edge may cover as much of the heading and turned-back tapestry as its width allows. Turn under the raw edges of the carpet binding.

With large, staggered back-stitches, stitch the carpet binding to the back of the tapestry along the inside edge and to the heading or turned-back portion of the tapestry along the outside edge. Use a sharp needle and high-quality cotton or silk quilting thread. To avoid distorting the weave, the stitches should penetrate only the back surface of the tapestry. Do not pull the stitches too tight or the tapestry will pucker. With a little practice and much checking of the right side of the tapestry, strong, invisible hand-stitches are possible. The wide, X-shaped stitches tack the edges of the carpet binding flush against the back of the tapestry and distribute the stress of the hem in a zigzag pattern.

The safest and most convenient way to mount a tapestry, rug, or other textile to a wall is with Velcro. Like carpet binding, Velcro comes in various widths. A small, lightweight tapestry can be mounted with Velcro as narrow as 1″ wide. Larger, heavier tapestries may require 2″- or 3″-wide Velcro (5 or 7.5 cm.). Because it is plastic, Velcro should not be attached directly to a

148

tapestry. It can, however, be securely machine-stitched to a length of carpet binding, which is then hand-stitched to the back of the tapestry.

First, select the appropriate width of Velcro for the size and weight of the tapestry, and cut the strips 1″ shorter than the top of the tapestry. If wide, heavy-duty Velcro is not available in your area, it is possible to support a large tapestry with two or three strips of the narrower width. Next, select a width of carpet binding about 1″ wider than the Velcro. The carpet binding should be washed, pressed, and cut about 3″ longer than the Velcro to allow for turning under its raw edges.

Center the length of fuzzy Velcro between the top, bottom, and sides of the carpet binding. Pin, then machine-stitch around all four edges of the Velcro. For very large, heavy tapestries, reinforce the bond between the Velcro and the carpet binding with two laps of machine stitching. With the raw edges of the carpet binding turned under, this mounting tape can be hand-stitched to the back of the tapestry, using the same crisscross back-stitches as the hems. Installed to a tapestry hem, the mounting tape replaces the carpet binding at that edge; installed along a selvedge, the mounting tape should overlap both finished hems.

Next, a corresponding length of Velcro must be mounted to the wall. First, cut a length of hardwood molding or one-by-two about 1″ shorter than the width of the top of the tapestry. Sand the wood and seal it with varnish or oil-base paint. Mount the wood to the wall in the correct position: Drill holes through the wood and into the wall, making a secure installation using screws, plastic plugs, masonry mounts, or whatever is appropriate for the wall surface. Take into consideration the size and weight of the tapestry and the extremely tenacious nature of the Velcro. Then, either staple or tack the prickly strip of Velcro onto the wood. This method of installing a tapestry, while being visually unobtrusive, allows for slight adjustments horizontally or vertically. The wood molding holds the back of the tapestry away from the wall. And, most important of all, the stress of the mounting is borne by the Velcro, not the warps or wefts of the tapestry.

Tapestry weavers who show their work in galleries can use a similar method for a temporary installation. Deliver the tapestry to the gallery attached by Velcro to a length of wood prepared in the same manner as for a permanent installation. Attached to the wood, the top of the tapestry is held flat and rigid. Monofilament can be tied around the wood to suspend the tapestry from the gallery's picture rail. And if the tapestry sells, the client can easily remove the wood and install it permanently.

Many weavers line their tapestries, for archival and aesthetic purposes. If the wall behind a tapestry has been painted with alkyd or other potentially caustic paint, a textile should not come into contact with it for any length of time. In addition, a lined tapestry has an additional barrier against deterioration from dust and air pollution. And, considering the appearance of the back of a tapestry, a lining neatly conceals the mass of weft tails and prevents their becoming magnets for the previously mentioned dust.

An excellent choice for a tapestry lining is a tightly woven, all-cotton fabric with a shiny surface to repel dust. As with anything that touches a tapestry permanently, remove any sizing by washing. Piece the lining if necessary and pin it to the back of the tapestry below the Velcro, turning under all four edges and mitering the corners. Hand-stitch it loosely, catching with the needle only the lining and the wefts on the back of the tapestry. Make sure that the tapestry is not buckled and that the stitches and the lining are not visible from the front.

A strip of Velcro attached to the back of a tapestry, and a corresponding strip attached to a mounting board.

Lining a tapestry. Photographed by Parklane Photo Labs.

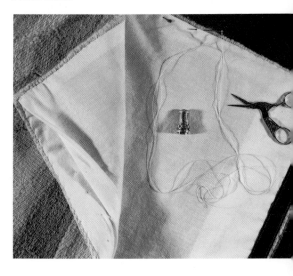

149

Even though a tapestry has been partially or completely steamed while damp, a second steaming is quite important. After the tapestry has been completely finished, steam it thoroughly using either an iron or a drapery steamer. An iron works only if the tapestry is lying horizontally, while a drapery steamer can be used vertically. This second steaming sets the tapestry hems and reinforces the setting of the wefts. Remember that the tapestry has been handled a great deal since its blocking. Also, the steaming of a blocked tapestry emphasizes the character of the weave by restoring the dimension and texture of the weft yarns. With a second steaming, a tapestry is finished in the most professional manner possible.

A tapestry mounted by a selvedge.

A finished tapestry. Photographed by Parklane Photo Labs.

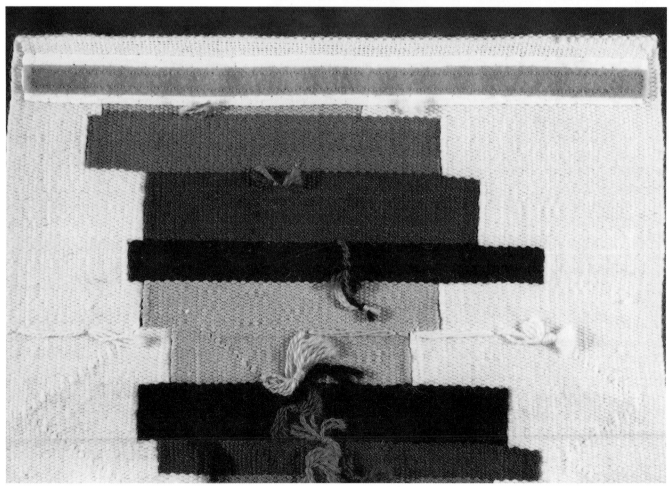

Designing for Tapestry

I s a cartoon the design for a tapestry? The answer is yes and no. A design is the artist's fully resolved plan for the two-dimensional images of a tapestry. It can be executed with watercolors, design markers, collage, or any other medium the artist prefers for translating nonvisual concepts into effective and weavable visual elements. A design need not be, nor is it usually, the same size as the tapestry. It should, however, accurately reflect the format of the tapestry and include all contour lines and proportions. And while each intricately hatched shading need not appear on a tapestry design, all shaded areas, as well as the distribution of critical values and hues, should be completely resolved to the artist's satisfaction before proceeding with the weaving.

A cartoon, on the other hand, is a simpler, more practical guide to the actual weaving of a tapestry. A cartoon is usually, but not always, the same size as the tapestry. It includes all contour lines, a guide to the placement of weft colors, and exact measurements of all lines and volumes to compare with woven measurements.

All tapestries should begin with a design, even those with simple geometric images. The design process ultimately establishes the visual elements of a tapestry. And the conviction that these elements and their interdependent relationships have been successfully arranged enables a weaver to confidently and accurately interpret them during the precious time at the loom. The costliest mistake a tapestry artist can make is a weak or poorly resolved design. Such designs result in many wasted weaving hours, as they can seldom be improved significantly by adjustments made during the interpretive process.

A small tapestry design worked in three value arrangements. Photographed by Parklane Photo Labs.

151

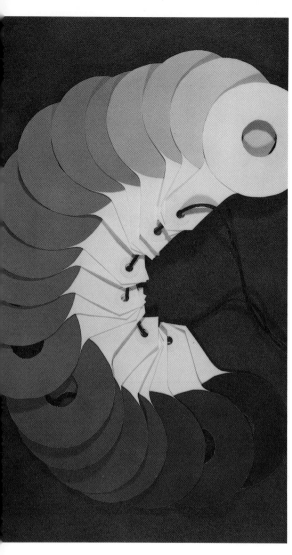

A value scale for matching color to value.
Photographed by Parklane Photo Labs.

Some tapestry artists begin the design process by assembling a collage of spontaneously torn design papers, adding outlines, shadings, or details with paint or marker pens. Others draft elaborate and studied compositions, using paint, pastels, or color pencils. Designers of geometric tapestries frequently plot precisely organized or symmetrical designs on graph paper that relates to the sett of the tapestry. Experience, personal preference, and complexity of image should influence a tapestry artist's choice of medium for design.

While developing an affinity for a particular medium is something to be aspired to by every artist, an understanding of the elements of two-dimensional design is the most valuable tool for making a successful translation from concept to tapestry. Consider the seven visual elements and their potential for expression in the medium of tapestry.

1. Value. Value refers to the relative lightness or darkness of a color. A graded scale for measuring values has two extremes, with white being the lightest and black being the darkest. Since all colors have value, they can be evaluated in terms of that characteristic by being compared with the gradation of grays between black and white.

In a tapestry, value can be expressed only with weft yarns. As explained throughout the text, value relationships between adjacent colors of weft yarns can either accentuate or modify the idiosyncracies of weft-crossing techniques. Furthermore, value relationships between blended or interpenetrating weft colors determine the visual effect of a shading technique. Therefore, a weaver must consider technique as well as value when combining weft colors for a tapestry design. But values for an actual tapestry, unlike those of the experimental sampler, should be carefully organized before beginning to weave.

Within a tapestry design, the element of value may affect factors other than technique, such as balance, distribution of light, form description, depth of space, and definition of shapes. But before attending to particular value contrasts, a designer should establish the tonality of a design by determining which values to include, according to one of six value keys. A value key, a general and rather flexible formula for stimulating a certain mood in a design, specifies the degree of contrast and the level of light. As in music, a value key may be either major or minor, referring to the degree of contrast. And within each of these two keys are three levels of illumination: light, middle, and dark. Therefore, the six possible value keys are: light major, middle major, dark major, light minor, middle minor, and dark minor.

Major value keys involve at least three highly contrasting values, including those from the very lightest and very darkest extremes of the value scale. Resolve such value arguments with a quantitative dominance of one general segment of the value scale. In other words, if a design has a high degree of value contrast, choose one of three dominant values: light, middle, or dark.

The light-major key involves contrasting values from all three segments of the value scale but with a dominance of lightest values. The tone established in a design with a light-major key is happy, lighthearted, and effervescent.

The middle-major value key is also highly contrasting but with a dominance of middle values. This key feels stronger and more stable with an easily read arrangement of values.

The dark-major value key has the same degree of contrast as the two other major keys but with a dominance of darkest values. This key, one of

152

The six value keys. Top row, left to right: light-major, middle major, and dark-major. Bottom row, left to right: light-minor, middle minor, and dark-minor. Photographed by Parklane Photo Labs.

prevailing darkness and heavy shadows, may seem threatening and tense.

Minor-value keys, contrasting much less than the major keys, involve closely related values from one segment of the value scale.

The light-minor value key includes only light, closely related values. Its tone is peaceful, positive, serene, and very delicate.

The middle-minor value key includes only closely related middle values. It reads as subdued, smoky, or foggy.

The dark-minor value key includes only closely related dark values. This difficult-to-work-with key is somber, weighty, and depressed.

I can suggest three methods for establishing a value key and all critical value relationships within a design. With experience, you may invent a few others. Designing for tapestry is a highly personal experience. And while the designing/refining process, whatever its medium, should be efficient and enjoyable, a beautiful, weavable design should always be the main focus.

The first method involves preparing a first draft for a design in values only, then refining the design, still in its gray stage, in terms of balance, composition, proportions, etc. This fully resolved value plan can be translated at that point into a medium involving hues. Color-Aid, Pantone, and other design papers are available in a wide range of grays. Design markers and pastels are also available in a range of values from black to white. Any of these media, combined with acrylic paint or drawing pencils, can be used to create a tapestry design in values.

Beginning with the actual colors envisioned for a tapestry is the second method of designing. In this approach, all colors (translated with paint, papers, pens, etc.) are established in the first draft, with careful consideration given to the distribution and proportions of light and dark areas. A second draft is subsequently created by translating the hues into their relative values. This draft provides an opportunity to fine-tune the design by adjusting the values lighter or darker as necessary.

The third method involves translating a design into more than one value key for the purpose of analyzing the different effects. Less experienced designers will find it enlightening to observe the drastic change of

The separation of light and dark from all appearance of colour is possible and necessary. The artist will solve the mystery of imitation sooner by first considering light and dark independently of colour, and making himself acquainted with it in its whole extent.

—Johann Wolfgang von Goethe

personality in a design brought about by adjusting its key. Furthermore, having settled on the optimum key for a design still allows for meddling with values. Try interchanging the heaviest or most crucial values in a design to find the arrangement that works best. For instance, without altering the key, switch the value of the background with the value of a large shape in the foreground. Or strengthen a composition by switching the values of two tiny shapes. Shifting shapes around or adjusting the values of elements in a design is an easy matter if you cut the individual shapes from design papers.

Values, the lights and shadows of a design, determine its tone and its inflections. Designing within the structure of a value key provides a scheme to guide the selection of weft colors and other design elements. And greater harmony of expression among all visual elements in the tapestry will be the result.

"The Red Wheelbarrow"

so much depends

upon

a red wheel

barrow

glazed with rain

water

beside the white

chickens

—*William Carlos Williams*

2. Color. Color is the favorite element of every tapestry weaver. For many of us, it is the primary reason for weaving. The deep, lively colors of weaving yarns stimulate creativity in a tactile person. For instance, a lustrous emerald silk yarn is a richer and more brilliant green than the jewel itself. And a sandy-beige handspun wool with tiny flecks of red, green, and black has the same quirky visual characteristics as the woven beach it becomes. Luminous red weft yarns glow with an intensity that makes painted flames appear pale in comparison to woven ones.

The element of color applies in a special way to a tapestry; the weft yarns contribute all color as well as other physical properties affecting color. In contrast to other types of handweaving, the warps in a tapestry never intrude, allowing unbroken gestures of expression with weft materials. Components of a design can be cut from paper, but the surface of the tapestry will have greater depth than the paper. A shape in a design can be colored with a marker pen, but the flat, transparent color of a pen cannot approximate the dense and lively color of the corresponding weft yarn. Therefore, when considering colors for a tapestry design, always consider actual weft yarns.

Some tapestry designers conceptualize in colors, envisioning clearly the hue, shade, or tint needed for interpreting an image—for instance, the peculiar shade of blue-green that the sea becomes right before a storm, or the unmistakable crimson of a poppy, or the foggy mauve and gray of late November. These artists may create an initial design in a medium with a limited range of colors—colors not corresponding exactly to the concept. But any inadequate colors in a tapestry design can be replaced in the weaving process with exact weft colors, ordered from a sample card or custom-dyed, restoring the brilliance of the original idea.

An alternative approach would be to design with the weft yarns available, allowing accessible colors to inspire and influence the design. High-quality tapestry wools are available in a wide range of colors from several yarn manufacturers. Added to these, an array of silks, linens, and perle cottons should satisfy nearly every color craving. But if there is one elusive color not carried by any yarn manufacturer, try blending it from several strands of analogous colors. Because of the optical interactions of its components, a blended color may turn out to be more interesting and successful than a solid one.

In a highly textured medium such as tapestry, each participating color has a strong voice. To avoid overwhelming a tapestry design, select colors carefully and according to a general plan. As with values, a plan to direct

154

the selection of colors guides and limits the design process. A hue circle—pure hues arranged in rainbow order—provides the basis for color planning. With this useful reference, you can plot geometric relationships between hues. The following are five approaches to the selection and organization of colors for a two-dimensional design:

Monochromatic. A monochromatic color plan involves a single hue. But derived from that single hue is a broad range of interesting contrasts. Take blue, for instance. Blue can be tinted to the lightest ice blue or shaded to the darkest ink; it can be as intense as electricity or as dull as faded denim. When considering a color for a tapestry design, consider its full potential of values, from the lightest to the darkest. Also consider a color's full range of intensities, from the brightest to the dullest.

Not all colors have a wide range of expressions within their specific hue. Some colors change character immediately as they shift away from the circle of pure hues. For instance, as red is tinted, it becomes pink; as orange is shaded, it becomes brown. Yellow tends to remain yellow only as a pure hue. A dark yellow is green or brown; a very pale yellow is cream. However, even though certain tints or shades deviate substantially from the central hue, a subliminal relationship exists, and they can be applied quite successfully to monochromatic designs as neutrals, backgrounds, shadows, or contrasts.

Analogous. An analogous approach to color planning involves two or three hues from a segment of the hue circle. For instance, yellow, orange, and red are analogous hues, as are green and blue, violet and red. Observe that the hues to one side of the circle are warm, while those to the other side are cool. Because analogous hues are taken from a limited arc of the hue circle, this color plan is characterized by a prevailing temperature. Yellow, orange, and red, all warm hues, cooperate to enhance a warm design. Green and blue are both cool. Even though green contains a warm component (yellow), the shared blue element dominates to produce a cool design. A design worked in violet and red would be warm, but not as hot as one containing a large proportion of yellow.

Direct complements. Every hue on the circle has a direct complement—the color directly opposite. The direct complement of yellow is violet. The direct complement of red/orange is blue/green. The direct complement of red is green. We seem to combine these colors instinctively, in life as well as art. Direct complements are the strongest color contrasts and may seem harsh and optically vibrating when combined as pure hues. But combined as tints or shades, they complete a harmonic chord. We respond to complementary colors in the same manner as we would respond to a harmony of diverse musical instruments. A delicate pink rose must be accompanied by a dark green leaf. A cobalt bowl is a requirement for storing fresh oranges. Fields of purple heather are usually sprinkled with bright goldenrod.

Triadic harmonies. Imagine placing a triangle over a hue circle, its points touching three of the hues. An equilateral triangle would touch three hues equidistant from each other. Red, blue, and yellow and yellow/orange, blue/green, and red/violet are two examples of triadic harmonies selected equilaterally. In each of these cases, the three colors function together in harmony by virtue of their three equal intervals.

I see contemporary tapestries as a way to give human, that is lyrical, scale to massive corporate architectural environment, and perchance to widen the horizon and heighten the awareness of human vitality, dignity and the inherent joy of life.

—Jan Yoors

155

Touching three colors on the hue circle with an isosceles triangle creates another type of triadic harmony, split complements. In other words, the triangle points to a color on one side of the circle (green) and its split complements (red/orange and red/violet) on the other side. Split complements—two hues to either side of the direct complement—provide broken and therefore less intense contrasts than direct complements.

Tetradic harmonies. A tetradic harmony involves four colors, selected by placing either a square or a rectangle over a hue circle. The corners of a square touch four hues with four equal intervals. The corners of a rectangle touch four hues with two sets of different but harmonious intervals. The two types of tetradic harmonies differ slightly from each other, but both methods organize four colors successfully. Tetradic harmonies are the most complicated color plans. If a tapestry design requires many colors, select and edit those colors according to a square or rectangular tetradic harmony.

A color plan for a tapestry design may be a simple, monochromatic arrangement of values of a single hue, a striking juxtaposition of complementary hues, or a complicated but organized network of contrasting hues. Recognize that each hue on the circle has a temperature and a full range of intensities; each hue can be tinted in steps to the lightest value or shaded in steps to the darkest. This seemingly endless number of color possibilities can be easily managed by preparing all designs for tapestries within a value key and according to a fundamental color plan.

3. Line. A tapestry artist's control of the element of line is not only crucial to the effective communication of concept, but also instrumental in the development of a distinctive personal style. Straight lines are the strongest type of lines and the most static and serene. But the inflexibility of an absolutely straight line may be too rigid for certain designs. Gently curved lines are more active and can be introduced singly or in a series, expressing a sensuous rhythm, a relaxed mood, or a positive emotion. But, used to excess in a tentative concept, curved lines may appear meandering or weak. Circles and spirals, changing direction abruptly, are more vigorous lines, lending enthusiasm or symbolism to a design. Because jagged lines convey much visual conflict, they are the most excited of all. However subliminally, we all recognize and respond to the characteristics of different types of lines. Applying lines effectively to a tapestry design requires only a bit of thought and organization before touching a pen or paper.

A tapestry design may include lines that are straight and crisp, curved and flowing, jagged and energetic, broken and sketchlike, or even dotted. While it is possible to weave all of these, most tapestry artists eventually develop a carefully edited, personal repertoire of certain types of woven lines. This limitation-by-choice is not a confinement of creativity but a mature refinement of an individual approach to tapestry design.

Woven lines, as a result of their interlacing of weft with warp, have a certain idomatic character, a character to be frankly exploited in the design process as well as in the weaving. To prepare a design for a tapestry, consider all lines very carefully. Straight vertical lines may require interlocking or sewing. Vertical curved lines must be constructed in steps along a series of warps and can be interpreted with crisp relays or feathered interlocks. Diagonal lines, to appear rigid and unwavering, must be

I watch people instinctively reach out to touch a wild creature in my tapestries . . . few mediums can invite that intimacy. Only then have I met my goal of bringing the viewer into the animal's life.

—Arlene Gawne

constructed with mathematical precision. Eccentric curved lines must be built up gradually from below. Jagged, irregular lines leap nervously from warp to warp and, more than any other type of woven line, owe their appearance to the textile structure. Outlines must be executed before, during, and after the weaving of the outlined shape. Further experience with tapestry technique will refine the technical execution of all types of woven lines; but the ultimate artistic refinement, to which we should all aspire, is a set of woven lines accurately corresponding to the designer's vision.

4. Direction. The element of direction (horizontal, vertical, diagonal, or a combination thereof) is usually established by the element of line. And as all lines have direction, the functions of the two are interdependent. A prevailing direction in a tapestry design can enhance a certain mood or emotion, strengthen the plausibility of a description of depth of space, anchor unstable elements in a composition, or convey movement.

Horizontal direction is established by a dominance of horizontal lines and can be further emphasized by placing the design within a horizontal format. Horizontal lines, similar in emotional effect to the horizontal surfaces on which we feel most secure, are balanced and stable. Design concepts associated with tranquility and serenity are most successfully expressed with this direction and in this format.

The vertical direction, while potentially the strongest and most positive, can lend an austere feeling to a design. Narrow portals are more mysterious and foreboding than wide entryways. In two-dimensional design, as in architecture, pairs of vertical lines introduce tension and strength, further enhanced by dominant vertical edges. The potency of the vertical direction can be appropriately applied to the expression of design concepts involving integrity, dignity, and aspiration.

The oblique or diagonal direction is the most active and can be exaggerated by frequent and irregular shifts of direction. The eyes of the viewer may be led into and through a lively design along a cleverly conceived trail of diagonals. A pair of divergent diagonals can be used to establish or frame the position of a focal point. And movement within a design, such as wind, is successfully expressed in a diagonal direction. A single, isolated diagonal line in a composition tilts precariously, requiring one or more opposite diagonals for stabilization and balance.

During the design process, a tapestry artist should evaluate the element of direction in relation to the following: the subject matter of the design and its intended impression on the viewer, the dominant types of lines involved in the design, the size and format of the tapestry, and, as always, the preferred design style of the artist.

5. Texture. There are two distinct types of texture: tangible and implied. Tangible texture exists in all woven work. It can be seen with your eyes and touched with your fingers. The shadows created in its crannies shift with the movement of light around it. Its depth is measurable. Implied texture, on the other hand, is perceivable only by the eyes. It may exist in any medium, even on the glossy, flat surface of a photograph. But unlike photographers or other visual artists, tapestry designers/weavers must concern themselves at all times with both types of textures.

Tangible texture in a tapestry cannot be avoided; it is created with each pass of the weft through the warps. The over-and-under actions of evenly spun weft yarns result in a regular, level woven surface that is characteristic

Spider Woman instructed the Navajo women how to weave on a loom which Spider Man told them how to make. The crosspoles were made of sky and earth cords, the warp sticks of sun rays, the heddles of rock crystal and sheet lightning. The batten was a sun halo, white shell made the comb. There were four spindles: one a stick of zigzag lightning with a whorl of cannel coal; one a stick of flash lightning with a whorl of turquoise; a third had a stick of sheet lightning with a whorl of abalone; a rain streamer formed the stick of the fourth, and its whorl was white shell.

—Navajo Legend

of most tapestry textures. To vary the fundamental texture of a tapestry, while introducing another rich and versatile visual element, expand your repertoire of weft yarns to include a selection of fine and medium-weight wool singles, textured wools and blends, silks, rayons, and perle cottons. Introduce these yarns alone or blend them with conventional wools in a tapestry design. Two impressive applications of textured weft yarns are Mona Elise Rummel's effervescent waves woven with a fine, loopy weft yarn and Arlene Gawne's strokable wild animals interpreted with chunky, handspun singles wool from Uruguay.

Blend in a few strands of lustrous weft yarns for another textural contrast. In comparison to light-absorbent wools, shiny silk and rayon yarns appear highly polished, splashed with sunlight, or even wet—imagine a silk puddle! Experiment with an area of soumak, twining, or chaining. Create a series of double weft interlocks, shifting the lumps intentionally to the front of the tapestry to create structural security and texture with the same technique.

These suggested approaches to creating tangible textures on a tapestry surface are extremely personal and must be selected and edited with care. A tangible texture can be introduced to express an artist's concept more fully or to emphasize a distinctive style of tapestry interpretation. Used skillfully and in the correct proportion, tangible textures and unconventional weft materials should not compromise a tapestry technically. A tapestry is, after all, a handwoven textile, and its structure and materials may be revealed frankly on its surface.

While tangible texture is a matter of personal preference, to be used or not at the discretion of the artist, implied textures must be managed by most tapestry weavers, even those preferring an uninterrupted tapestry surface. Implied texture describes the surface of an image within the design. For instance, a brick wall in a tapestry design can be woven with the same evenly spun weft yarns as the flat, blue sky behind it. Touching the wall reveals the same relatively flat tapestry surface as the sky. But the wall appears to have deep fissures and a very rough, uneven, and occasionally sharp texture. This visual texture is created with weft yarns of consistent quality but contrasting values and intensities.

Examine the various textures in the tapestries throughout the book. Then observe how the artists created this element in their own unique ways. The hues, values, and intensities of the weft yarns involved are essential to the successful simulation of texture, as is the technique by which the weft colors are interwoven. Pick-and-pick, dots, stripes, hatchings, and blended wefts, woven with contrasting weft yarns, can all be applied to simulate textures in a tapestry design. Textures, tangible or implied, enrich a tapestry, clarify relationships, contribute patterns, and, most of all, integrate harmoniously with an unavoidably textured art form.

6. Shape. The element of shape is closely related to the elements of line and proportion. Shapes are described with contour lines, while the two-dimensional measurements of shapes determine key proportions in a design. A contour line may separate a shape from a background area or travel between adjacent shapes. Therefore, with the element of line an artist determines the size and configuration of all shapes in a design—even the shapes of the negative areas. Negative areas should never be designed by default; their shapes and dimensions have a significant impact on the resolution of the design.

The shapes in a representational design communicate their identities to the viewer, but they also speak of the unique perceptions of the tapestry artist. Each of us perceives a tree or any common, recognizable shape according to our own special sensitivities. The shapes in a representational tapestry design should reflect these sensitivities.

A striking geometric design includes universally recognizable shapes, but their sizes, colors, and intervals are composed to deliver an artist's singular message or sense of unity. An abstract design involves ambiguous shapes, describing less accessible aspects of a concept while demanding an interaction with the viewer's perception.

Some familiar shapes have deep-rooted metaphorical connotations that may describe or emphasize emotions and concepts not easily translated into visual terms. For instance, symbolic associations of a circle include expressions of universal or personal wholeness, unity, the earth, the sun, the moon, a mandala, a ring, and the essence of femininity. A triangle, depending upon its proportions or context, may symbolize stable, positive, three-way concepts or it may appear flamelike and threatening, symbolizing negative masculine principles such as volcanic behavior, restlessness, and aggression. Birds (the dove of peace), animals (the caduceus, a staff with two entwined snakes and two wings at the top), flowers (the rose, symbol of love), and trees (an olive branch) may all have symbolic potential. Symbolic shapes can be central to a design or they can be relegated to a secondary, subliminal function. In either case, shapes within a design have the potential to become compelling symbols

7. Proportion. A design for a tapestry should be well proportioned. In other words, each visual element within a tapestry design should be neither too large nor too small in relation to the other elements and to the overall size and format of the tapestry. Since the time of Euclid, proportions or ratios for architecture and two-dimensional design have been assigned (and argued about) according to rigid mathematical formulas. But more flexible and adaptable proportions can be established by dividing the surface of a design according to the principles of variation and unity.

Variation refers to a design's contrasting elements. For a design to be interesting, contrast of some degree must be present. Unity refers to the proportional resolution of contrasting elements. A unified design must include one element proportionately larger than the others—a quantitative dominance. The dominant element may be a single shape or repetition of a shape, a line or repetition of a line, a color, or any visual element that quantitatively dominates the other (subordinate) elements.

Contrasts in a design can occur between any of the visual elements; unification always involves the element of proportion. For instance, two flowers may be related in shape and size but contrasting in color and value—a potentially interesting but unresolved composition. Improve this design by adjusting its proportions according to one of two approaches. The first would be to increase the size of one of the flowers. The second would be to add more flowers of one color. In either case, the design is unified by a quantitative dominance of one element. Another example is two rectangles, related in line, shape, and direction (both rectangles are vertical), but contrasting in implied texture, color, and value (one is a brick building, the other stucco). To resolve the contrasts and unify the design, allow one of the buildings to dominate the other.

The other aspect of craft work is concerned with art work, the realization of a hope for a lawful and enduring nature. Other elements, such as proportion, space relations, rhythm, predominate in these experiments, as they do in other arts. No limitations other than the veto of the material itself are set. More than an active process, it is a listening for the dictation of the material and a taking in of the laws of harmony. It is for this reason that we can find certitude in the belief that we are taking part in an eternal order.

—Anni Albers

Proportion is the key to the unification of a design. If a design seems unsettling or unresolved, analyze its elements and adjust their proportions. Experiment with expanding or reducing the proportions of negative areas. Scrutinize a design from all four directions. A unified design includes the right number of elements, with each element the right size for that particular design.

Making and handling a cartoon. Once a tapestry design is complete, the next step is to enlarge it to cartoon dimensions. While it is possible—even preferable, in the case of small tapestries—to design full-scale, a more practical approach is to make a maquette (a small design) and expand it to the size of the tapestry.

Some weavers make a cartoon by projecting their maquette from an opaque projector onto a large sheet of paper taped to a wall. With this method it is important to check for distortion of the image by measuring all four edges of the tapestry design as it is projected onto the paper. The two vertical edges should be exactly the same length, as should the two horizontal edges. The angles of all four corners should be 90°. If your square or rectangular format has become a parallelogram or trapezoid, distortion of the image has occurred in the projection. And if the borders of a design are distorted, interior contours will be also. Adjust the angle of the projector and the position of the maquette to correct any distortions.

A slide projector can be used in a similar manner to project a slide of the maquette. To make an undistorted slide, the lens of the camera must be perfectly parallel to the design. This requires a steady hand, a tripod, or a "copy camera." A copy camera, available through certain photographers or photo labs, is bolted to a rack, its lens pointing downward toward a level

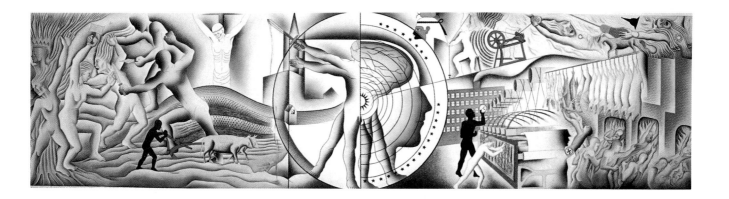

table. The camera can be focused, raised, or lowered without altering the parallel relationship between the lens and the table. With the maquette lying flat on the table, the photographer can shoot an undistorted image of it. However, as with an opaque projector, check for distortions in projection.

Both projection processes permit you to view full-scale the visual elements of your future tapestry. Enlarging its proportions points out any flaws or weaknesses in a design, and viewing it from the perspective of the weaver (usually sideways) enables you to evaluate its weavability. Use this opportunity to examine your design from both perspectives—that of the viewer and that of the weaver—and then make any adjustments.

Allow sufficient time to trace the design all at once. It would be nearly impossible to reset either type of projector in exactly the same position. Use a pencil to trace the contour lines and the edges of the tapestry. When all lines have been traced, again check the design and make any final adjustments. When the cartoon is completed to your satisfaction, darken the lines with a marker.

Next, measure all crucial lengths, widths, and intervals within the design, marking these measurements on the cartoon. To appear in the completed tapestry as you intended, all woven shapes and intervals must correspond closely in length and width to those on the cartoon. Having all measurements at hand provides a convenient reference during the weaving process.

There are other methods for expanding a maquette. And while most of them do not provide an opportunity to view a potential tapestry full-scale, they permit an artist/weaver complete control over the enlarging of its design.

A venerable, but still widely used, technique for expanding a design is the grid method. This method requires tracing a small-scale grid over the maquette and a larger-scale grid onto the paper to be used for the cartoon. The squares may be any size, but they should be perfectly square, and both grids should have the same number of squares. Because the maquette is divided into small squares, its curved lines and intervals can be accurately expanded according to the positions of the corresponding squares on the cartoon.

Some experienced tapestry artists never make a full-scale cartoon. A small tapestry design on graph paper, prepared according to the artist's predetermined scale and proportions, contains all the information needed for translating the design into woven form. The spaces between the vertical lines of the graph paper refer to a certain number of warps, while the spaces between the horizontal lines refer to a certain number of weft passes.

Audrey Cowan and I have been working together for 15 years. We first met during The Dinner Party, *when Audrey wove the tapestry section of the runner for Eleanor of Aquitaine. I had never designed for weaving before* The Dinner Party, *but had become intrigued by the way the wool translated and softened my images.*

I particularly liked working with Audrey because she had the skill and visual acuity to be able to interpret my cartoons and bring them alive. We have a very open and honest working relationship—I entrust Audrey with my painted image and trust her to translate it into the technique she's adept at. I want her to bring her whole self into the work—her ideas, her values, her skills. Only then do I feel the finished work is the product of two people—the artist and the weaver. (We own the work we do jointly.) As I have often told her, "If I wanted a robot, I'd look for a machine." I am completely opposed to reducing a person to an automaton, and I don't think one gets the best work from a weaver (or craftsperson of any kind) unless one provides space for that person to bring their own point of view to the work. —Judy Chicago

161

The 17th of October 1989 changed me. I live and work in San Francisco.

Two days after the earthquake, with a path cleared through the glass in my house, I sorted through my broken china and found two cups that could be reconstructed. I painted them, over and over again, trying to put them together.

From the University of California, I received, as requested, a copy of the seismograph of the earthquake. To see it represented on a graph was powerful: a thin line destroying lives, freeways, property, and my china cups.

A fine line—in the aftershock I began to weave.   —Constance Hunt

Above: Aftershock, *tapestry by Constance Hunt, along with the cartoon from which it was woven. Left: detail. Cotton warp, wool weft; 12″ x 18″ (30 by 45 cm.); 1990. Photo: Gary Hunt.*

Above: Kodalith cartoon for Susan Guagliumi's El color es la canción Mexicana y todo el pueblo canta. *Right: detail of tapestry. Linen warp, wool Swedish singles weft; 51″ x 68″ (128 by 170 cm.); 1983. Photo: Arthur Guagliumi.*

Therefore, shifting weft colors from warp to warp, according to the vertical guides of the grid, develops accurate contour lines; counting weft passes develops the volume of shapes vertically. This method of woven interpretation is especially useful if a design is quite simple or if it is symmetrical or geometric.

Because a cartoon is handled and stabbed with pins during the tapestry-making process, it must be reinforced before it becomes perforated or torn. Reinforce all four edges of the cartoon with wide masking tape. Then tape the cartoon randomly from side to side and top to bottom several times. These additional tapes halt the progression of any rips while providing reinforced areas for pinning.

163

Next, assign colors of weft yarns to the sections of the cartoon. One method is to tape strands of weft directly to the corresponding shape on the cartoon. Another method is to make a note of the yarn manufacturer's color number on the cartoon.

At this point, make certain that you have enough weft material for weaving the entire tapestry. Imagine running out of that perfect blue yarn before your sky is finished! To determine how much weft yarn is required to weave one square inch, weigh a small tapestry or sample having the same sett and proportion of weft as the tapestry you intend to weave. Then divide its weight (in ounces) by the number of square inches in the piece. The result will be the weight of weft yarn (in ounces) needed to weave one square inch. For instance, a small tapestry sample sett at six ends-per-inch, woven with a six-strand weft, measures 9" x 27" (22.5 x 67.5 cm.), for an area of 243 square inches (1518.75 sq. cm.), and weighs eight ounces. Therefore, one square inch of a tapestry of this quality requires approximately .033 ounces of yarn. In a similar tapestry, a sky measuring 100 square inches would require at least 33 ounces of blue weft yarn.

The best method for handling a cartoon during the weaving process depends greatly upon the type and size of your loom. For instance, the entire width of the warp on a narrow (60" or less) horizontal loom can be reached from one side or the other, permitting easy access for pinning a cartoon to the fell. With this type of loom the cartoon can be pinned (diaper pins or T-pins work well) to the hem at the beginning of the tapestry and repinned upward as the weaving progresses. The contour lines can be traced onto the warps, as in your sampler, or they can be followed directly from the cartoon, positioned conveniently below the weaving.

Wider horizontal looms require a rack of some sort to hold the cartoon below the warps and to facilitate the advancing of the fell. In either case, never roll the cartoon around the front beam under the tapestry. A cartoon pinched between the tapestry and the beam will tear under the strain. And if the position of the cartoon were to shift slightly, it would be impossible to adjust it under a tensioned tapestry. The cartoon should be attached only by the row of pins.

Some vertical looms have a rod for holding a cartoon behind the warps. If your loom has no rod, a strong cord can be installed between the vertical supports and the cartoon pinned to, or suspended from, the cord. If you prefer to translate the tapestry directly from the cartoon, pin it to the fell to hold it close to the weaving. Otherwise, as the weaving progresses, pin the cartoon to the warps each time you need to trace lines.

A cartoon is a valuable tool for a tapestry artist. It prescribes fundamental relationships between the visual elements of a tapestry design, and it guides the evolution of contours and volumes. Working within the guidelines of a cartoon, a weaver has a reassuring sense of the beginning, the middle, and the end of a shape. But a tapestry need not conform rigidly to its guide, and a mere cartoon should not intrude upon the preeminent relationship between the weaver and the weaving. For a tapestry to become high art—to truly come to life—the heart and mind of its maker must be present in every thread. As your tapestry grows, inch by inch, participate fully in its creation, infusing it with your spirit and molding it with your hands. Allow a certain spontaneity of color and flexibility of interpretation. From time to time, stand back and let your tapestry breathe and speak for itself. Trust your judgment, enjoy yourself every step of the way, and your tapestries will sing.

This tapestry was inspired by "The Precious Legacy," an exhibition at the Royal Ontario Museum in 1985. The exhibition featured treasures and religious artifacts from the oldest Jewish community of Europe.

From 1942 to 1945, the Nazis deported Jews to captivity and death, confiscated their possessions of historical value, and shipped the artifacts to Prague to establish a "museum to an extinct race."

Included in the exhibit were one small leather suitcase, closed, with numbers on it, and a photograph of a deportation scene—a young boy and an older man pulling a cart with two leather suitcases containing their personal possessions.

—Sylvia Ptak

Cartoon for Sylvia Ptak's 1941—Baggage, Destination Unknown, #2. Paint, paper, and photographs; 10″ x 7″ (25 by 18 cm.). Photo: Jack Ramsdale.

Sylvia Ptak, 1941—Baggage, Destination Unknown, #2. Linen warp, wool weft with accents of mohair, acrylic, metallic threads, and chenille; 57″ x 46″ (143 by 115 cm.); 1989. Photo: Michael Courtney.

Elaine Ireland, Leaning Corinthian. *Cotton warp, wool and cotton floss weft; 44″ x 44″ (110 by 110 cm.); 1985. The design element "direction."*

Arlene Gawne, Evening Hunt. *Cotton warp, wool weft; 30″ x 60″ (75 by 150 cm.). The design elements "value" and "shape."*

DESIGNING FOR TAPESTRY

Victor Jacoby, Afternoon Shadows. *Cotton warp, wool weft; 32″ x 30″ (80 by 75 cm.); 1989. Photo: James D. Toms. The design element "color."*

Mona Elise Rummel, Cannon Beach *(detail). Cotton warp, wool weft with accents of silk, rayon, and mohair; 24″ x 29″ (60 by 73 cm.); 1980. The design element "texture."*

167

Joyce Hulbert, Icon. Wool warp, hand-dyed wool weft; 42″ x 66″ (105 by 165 cm.); 1989. The design element "proportion."

Jan Yoors, Fighting Stallions. Woven by Annabert and Marianne Yoors. Cotton warp, wool weft; 72″ x 72″ (180 by 180 cm.); 1956. Photo: George Cserna. The design element "line."

DESIGNING FOR TAPESTRY

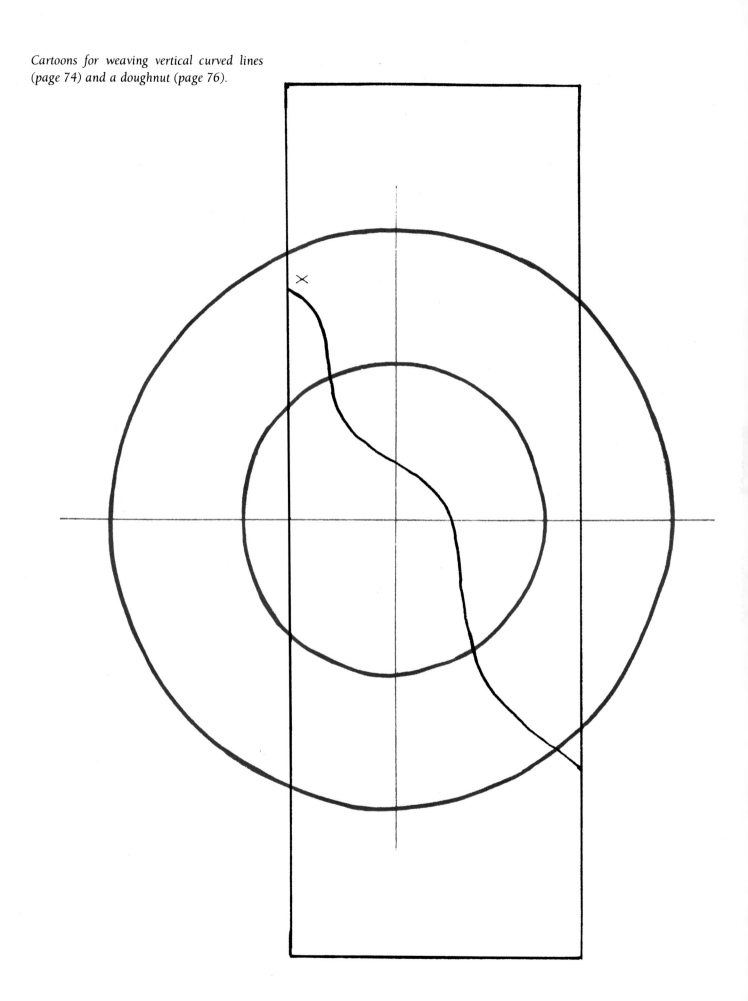

Cartoons for weaving vertical curved lines (page 74) and a doughnut (page 76).

Glossary

Acrylic loop yarn: Several removable picks of this fine, fuzzy, inexpensive yarn temporarily secure the first and last picks of a tapestry heading or other weaving project.

Alternation: Repeated interchange of two visual elements.

Apron: A length of canvas or several lengths of twill tape attached to the warp and cloth beams of a loom. An apron holds one or two sturdy metal or wooden apron rods. The end of a warp would be tied to the apron rod on the warp beam of a loom, and the beginning of a warp would be tied to the apron rod on the cloth beam.

Aubusson: A French tapestry workshop, originally located in the region of central France known as La Marche; also frequently used to indicate tapestries woven on low-warp looms with treadles.

Back beam: The beam or rail at the extreme rear of the loom.

Background: In a tapestry design, the term refers to the negative space between the figures.

Basse lisse: A low-warp loom.

Bast fibers: Woody fibers from plants, including jute, hemp, flax (linen), and sisal.

Batten: The beater on a floor or table loom; also, a flat, smooth, sword-shaped stick used to hold the shed open on a vertical tapestry loom and to pack the weft.

Beaming: Winding a warp onto the warp beam of a loom.

Beat: To pack weft yarn into a shed.

Beater: On a loom, a beater is the swinging beam that holds the reed and beats weft into the shed. See **Comb**.

Bight: A specified number of warps knotted onto an apron rod. The number of warps in a bight usually relates to the sett. For instance, a warp sett at six ends per inch would be knotted in bights of six.

Block: To carefully apply moisture to a tapestry and then dry it very slowly, resulting in a fixed, even woven surface.

Bobbin: A tube or spool designed to fit into a shuttle and release its supply of weft yarn as needed. Bobbins may be plastic, wood, or paper. Refer to **Tapestry Bobbin** for another definition.

Bobbin winder: An electric or manual accessory for winding weft yarn onto a bobbin.

Breast beam: The front rail or beam on a loom.

Bubbling: Introducing a slight excess of weft yarn into a shed by hand. A row of weft is directed intermittently into the top of the previous row, resulting in a series of weft semicircles or "bubbles."

Butterfly: A length of yarn wound around the fingers and secured with a knot. A butterfly provides a small source of weft yarn for tapestry weaving.

Cartoon: A tapestry design painted or drawn to full scale.

Castle: The part of the loom frame from which the harnesses are suspended.

Chain: A series of continuous loops, similar to a crochet chain, made in a warp as it is pulled from the warping board. The purpose of a chain is to temporarily shorten the length of the warp for easier handling.

Chain spacer: A row of continuous loops used to establish and secure the spacing of a warp on a loom with no reed.

Cloth beam: The front roller on a loom onto which the woven fabric is wound.

Comb: A fork-shaped hand tool used by tapestry weavers to beat rows of weft.

Complements: Two colors from opposite extremes of the hue circle which, when mixed together in the correct proportion, result in a neutral or gray tone; for example, red/green, violet/yellow, blue/orange, and red-orange/blue-green.

Concept: The message within the design expressed by its visible elements.

Counterbalanced loom: A loom designed to lower one set of harnesses as the opposite harnesses are raised.

Cross: Refers to the crisscrossing of the warp threads while winding them. A cross serves to retain the order of the warps as the loom is threaded.

Dents: The open spaces in the reed through which the warp threads pass. When used with a number, dent refers to the openings per inch in the reed.

Design: The plan for a textile or tapestry—its format, organization, proportions, color relationships, etc. A successful design must include contrasting elements, unified by a quantitative dominance of a single element.

Direction: A very important part of any design. Created with color, line, texture, value, or pattern, direction may be predominantly vertical, horizontal, or diagonal.

Dog: On a loom, a dog (or ratchet catch) serves as a brake while releasing the tension on a warp or moving it forward, the same as pawl.

Dominance: While not necessarily the focal point of a design, dominance is a visual element that quantitatively, not qualitatively, unifies and resolves its contrasts.

Dovetail: A technique for reversing the directions of two adjacent wefts around a common warp, producing a secure, horizontal crossing of the wefts.

Drawing in: A gradual shrinking of the width of a woven piece.

Dressing the loom: Installing a warp onto a loom.

Eccentric: A term applied to wefts that deviate from the usual horizontal relationship to the warp.

Edging cord: Plied cords caught in the selvedges of a Navajo rug for additional strength and reinforcement.

Elements: The visible factors in a design.

End: (verb) To delete a weft from a tapestry while invisibly securing its tail.

Ends: The individual warp threads.

Enter: To introduce a weft into a tapestry while invisibly securing its tail.

E. P. I.: Ends per inch; refers to the sett of the warp.

Fell: The position of the last pick of a weaving in progress.

Fiber: The material from which yarn is spun.

Filling: The weft.

Finger-hank: See **Butterfly**.

Finishing: The process of blocking and hemming a tapestry after it has been removed from the loom.

Fiskgarn: A tightly twisted cotton cord, commonly used for making fishing nets; an excellent warp yarn for tapestries or rugs. The same as seinetwine or seine-cotton.

Float: A skip of the weft over two or more warps, or a skip of the warp over two or more wefts. The same word applies to planned skips as well as to mistakes in the weave.

Form description: A planned gradation of hue, intensity, value, or any combination thereof, portraying round-ness or volume.

Frame loom: The simplest type of loom. Its only function is to hold warps in a stretched and parallel condition. On a frame loom, all other weaving manipulations must be executed by hand.

Gobelin: A French tapestry workshop; also traditional flat-woven tapestry or interlocking wefts. A Gobelin-style loom is a vertical tapestry loom with roller beams and hand-manipulated yarn heddles.

Gradation: A stepped sequence of one or more visual elements.

Hachures: (noun) See **Hatch** and **Hatching**. In this text, hachures refer to a formal, organized approach to the technique.

Half-pass: One pick—a single row of weaving. Tapestry requires two picks for each complete pass.

Half-tone: An intermediate color between two contrasting values or hues.

Hank: Similar to a skein.

Harmonious: Refers to visual elements that are similar.

Harness: On a loom, a harness is the frame used to raise or lower certain groups of warp threads. The same as shaft.

Hatch: (verb) To create interpenetrating lines or triangles of contrasting, adjacent weft colors.

Hatchings: The same as hachures. Used in this text to describe the less formal style of the technique.

Haute lisse: A high-warp loom.

Heading: Several tightly woven rows of plain weave at the beginning and end of a tapestry.

Heddle: A wire or string with an eye through which the warp threads pass.

Hem: A heading intended to be turned under as a finished edge.

High-warp: A tapestry loom on which the warp yarns are stretched vertically.

Hue: The common name of any color; or a pure color, one that has not been lightened, darkened, or reduced in intensity.

Hue circle: A more precise term than color wheel; a progression of pure hues organized around a circle.

Intensity: The brightness or purity of a color.

Interlace: To interweave weft yarns with a warp to make a textile.

Interlock: To cross adjacent wefts between warps; also a noun referring to the crossing procedure.

Inversion: An exact reversal of the previous order of elements.

Jack-type loom: A loom designed to raise certain harnesses by depressing pedals.

Kilim: A weft-face, flat-woven rug or other textile, completely reversible, involving the slit tapestry technique.

Lams: Parts of a floor loom to which the harnesses are tied from above and the treadles are tied from below. The same as marches.

Lazy line: A subtle, textural line traveling through the background of certain tapestries and Navajo rugs. A lazy line is created by a diagonal pattern of relays executed by two wefts of the same color.

Lease sticks: Two smooth sticks, placed through either side of the cross of a warp, used to keep the alternating warp threads in order during the threading process.

Lever: Levers mounted on the castle of a table loom raise or lower the harnesses.

Limn: To outline.

Loft: The height or resiliency of a yarn.

Low-warp: A loom on which the warps are stretched horizontally.

Luster: The gloss or sheen of a fiber.

Maquette: A small-scale design.

Marches: See **Lams**.

Modeling: A technique involving a gradation of values, describing volume or illumination.

Modulate: To move gradually, in small successive steps, between contrasting elements. For instance, one could modulate between extremes of value, hue, or intensity. Or, one could modulate with graded intervals between an area of deep texture and one which is absolutely flat.

Monochromatic: Several values of the same hue.

Navajo rug: A flat-woven, weft-face wool rug. The design of a Navajo rug is usually balanced and geometric, with simple color organization. It is woven on a continuous warp resulting in four selvedges.

Niddy-noddy: A hand reel used for winding skeins.

Ombre: Carefully graded stripes used to shade from one hue or value to another.

Pass: (noun) In tapestry weaving, a complete pass requires two picks.

Pawl: See **Dog**.

Pedals: See **Treadles**.

Pick: A single throw of the shuttle or butterfly carrying the weft through a shed. The same meaning as row or shot.

Pick-and-pick: The technique of weaving two contrasting colors of weft into separate, alternating sheds, resulting

Glossary

in narrow vertical stripes.

Pick-up stick: A flat, smooth stick used to separate and lift alternate warps, creating a shed.

Plain weave: A weave in which the weft passes over odd numbered warps in one shed and even numbered warps in the alternate shed. Technically, plain weave is the same as tabby and tapestry, although the term tapestry implies a weft-face textile.

Ply: To twist together two or more yarns for additional strength.

Pointillism: A technique of painting (or weaving) an area of tiny dots of contrasting colors not intended by the artist to be perceived individually. From a distance, pointillist dots interact to create shimmering colors in the eyes and mind of the viewer.

P. P. I.: Picks per inch. Refers to the number of rows of wefts per inch of weaving.

Primary: The three primary colors are red, blue, and yellow.

Progression: An orderly sequence of visual elements.

Proportion: The relationship of measurements.

Pull-shed: On a Navajo loom, the pull-shed is created by pulling on a stick tied to every other warp. On a Gobelin-style tapestry loom, the pull-shed is created by pulling the yarn heddles.

Raddle: A toothed tool used to keep the warps evenly distributed during the beaming process.

Ratchet: The serrated wheels on the front and back rollers of a loom, into which a pawl catches, permitting motion of a beam in one direction only.

Rayon: A natural cellulose fiber processed from wood.

Reed: The removable part of the beater which spaces the warp and packs the weft.

Reed hook: A flat, S-shaped hook used to draw warps through the dents of the reed.

Relay: The actions of tapestry wefts as they reverse directions around adjacent warps.

Rising shed: An opening in the warp created as certain harnesses are lifted by jacks or levers. The opposite of a sinking shed.

Secondary: The secondary colors are orange, violet, and green.

Seinetwine: See **Fiskgarn.**

Selvedge: The outside edge of a textile.

Selvedge warps: The two warps at the extreme right and left edges of the weaving.

Sett: The number of warp threads per inch.

Shade: (verb) To darken a color by the addition of black or gray. (noun) A darker, less intense form of the pure hue.

Shading: A shading in a design refers to areas that have been gradually darkened or lightened to convey illumination, depth of space, or form.

Shaft: The same as harness.

Shed: The opening in the warp through which the weft passes.

Shot: One row of weaving; the same as row or pick.

Shuttle: A shuttle holds a supply of weft yarn and carries it through a shed. Over the years, craftsmen have invented many different types of shuttles for various weaving purposes. Tapestry weavers frequently use the simplest shuttle of all—a butterfly.

Shuttle race: On a loom, the shuttle race is the protruding ledge in front of the reed on the beater.

Singles: Yarn that is not plied.

Sinking shed: An opening in the warp created by drawing down one or more harnesses. The opposite of rising shed.

Skein: A measured amount of yarn wound into a circular hank, then tied and twisted to keep the strands in order.

Sleying: Threading the warp ends through the dents of a reed.

Slit: A pair of adjacent interior selvedges in the woven structure of a tapestry or rug, caused by relaying adjacent weft yarns around the same two warps several passes in succession.

Soumak: An ancient technique for knotting wefts around warps to produce a textured, firm-surface textile.

Stick-shed: On a Navajo or Gobelin-style tapestry loom, the stick-shed is opposite the pull-shed. Above the pull-shed, a dowel or stick holds the stick-shed slightly open. Into this opening, a pick-up stick may be inserted and turned on end to create the stick shed.

Swift: An umbrella-like tool used for holding skeins of yarn while winding balls or shuttles.

Tabby: Plain weave, or tapestry weave. Also, a shed with alternate warps lowered.

Take-up: The contraction of the warp yarn caused by the interlacing of warp and weft.

Tapestry beater: See **Comb.**

Tapestry bobbin: A bobbin used to hold a small supply of weft yarn for tapestry weaving. Tapestry bobbins may have rounded or pointed ends.

Tapestry loom: A vertical or high-warp loom.

Tapestry weaving: The interweaving of individual, discontinuous weft yarns with tensioned warp yarns, through two alternate sheds, resulting in a weft-surface textile constructed simultaneously with its patterns or images.

Tertiary: The range of neutral colors produced by modulating between two secondary colors.

Textile: A woven, knit, crocheted, or felted cloth. Into this category would fall rugs, tapestries, garments, household linens, and fabrics.

Texture: The surface quality of a textile.

Threading: Drawing the warp ends through the heddle eyes according to a draft, repeat, or pattern.

Threading hook: A small hook used to draw the warp threads through the heddles.

Thrums: The unweavable ends of the warps tied to the back apron rod.

Tie-up: (verb) To link the harnesses to the treadles. (noun) The combinations of harnesses used in a weaving pattern.

Tint: (verb) To lighten the value of a hue. (noun) A tint is a lighter, less intense value of a hue.

Tone: (verb) To break the intensity of a pure hue with the addition of gray or the complementary hue. (noun) A grayed, less intense color.

Transparency: An illusion of one seemingly transparent color partially overlapping a second, opaque color. Key to the success of such an illusion is a sufficient proportion of the overlapping colors and a plausible, intermediate color between them.

Treadle: On a floor loom, treadles are used to direct the action of the harnesses.

Treadling: The sequence in which the harnesses or combination of harnesses are raised.

Twining: A method of wrapping pairs of wefts around the warps. Sometimes used as a warp spacer on a tapestry loom.

Value: The relative lightness or darkness of a hue.

Warp: The threads stretched vertically on a loom.

Warp beam: The roller on the back of a loom, onto which the warp is wound.

Warp chain: A prepared warp, at hand for dressing the loom. The warp threads have been crossed to retain their order, measured, counted, and looped into a chain.

Warp-face: A dominant proportion of warp in a woven structure, resulting in a textile in which the weft is completely covered by the densely packed warp.

Warp sticks: Sticks placed between layers of warp as it is wound onto the warp beam. Their purpose is to control the winding process, keeping the tension even as the warp is wound and unwound.

Warping board: A pegged board for making warps of 15 yards or less.

Warping reel: A framelike device that turns on a center spindle and is used for winding longer warps.

Weaving: Interlacing warp and weft threads to create a textile.

Weaving space: The accessible warps between the fell and the reed.

Web: The woven cloth.

Weft: The horizontal threads crossing the width of the warp.

Weft crossing: A technique for securely joining adjacent wefts either around a common warp or in a space between two warps.

Weft-face: A dominant proportion of weft in a woven structure, resulting in a dense, heavy textile with completely covered warps.

Weft tail: The cut end of a tapestry weft, which must be secured into the structure of the textile in some manner.

Woof: Synonym for weft; no longer commonly used.

173

Bibliography

Tapestry: Background and Techniques

Albers, Anni. *On Weaving*. Middletown, CT: Wesleyan University Press, 1965.

Bennett, Noel and Tiana Bighorse. *Working With the Wool: How to Weave a Navajo Rug*. Flagstaff, AZ: Northland Press, 1971.

Beutlich, Tadek. *The Technique of Woven Tapestry*. London: B. T. Batsford; New York: Watson-Guptill, 1967.

Brostoff, Laya. *Weaving a Tapestry*. Loveland, CO: Interweave Press, 1982.

Collingwood, Peter. *The Techniques of Rug Weaving*. London: Faber and Faber; New York: Watson-Guptill, 1968.

Constantine, Mildred and Jack Lenor Larson. *Beyond Craft: The Art Fabric*. New York: Van Nostrand Reinhold, 1972.

D'Harcourt, Raoul. *Textiles of Ancient Peru and Their Techniques*. Seattle: University of Washington Press, 1962.

Emery, Irene. *The Primary Structures of Fabrics: An Illustrated Classification*. Washington, DC: The Textile Museum, 1980.

Forman, B. and W. with Ramses Wissa Wassef. *Tapestries From Egypt: Woven by the Children of Harrania*. Prague: Artia; London: Paul Hamlyn, 1961.

Hall, Joanne. *Mexican Tapestry Weaving*. Helena, MT: J. Arvidson Press, 1976.

Harvey, Nancy. *The Guide to Successful Tapestry Weaving*. Seattle: Pacific Search Press, 1981.

Harvey, Nancy. *Patterns for Tapestry Weaving: Projects and Techniques*. Seattle: Pacific Search Press, 1984.

Harvey, Virginia I. and Harriet Tidball. *Weft Twining*. Lansing, MI: The Shuttlecraft Guild, 1969.

Jarry, Madeleine. *World Tapestry: From Its Origins to the Present*. France: Librairie Hachette; New York: G. P. Putnam's Sons, 1968.

Kybalová, Ludmila. *Contemporary Tapestries From Czechoslovakia*. Prague: Artia; London: Allan Wingate, 1963.

Mattera, Joanne. *Navajo Techniques for Today's Weaver*. New York: Watson-Guptill, 1975.

Pearson, Alec. *The Complete Book of Tapestry Weaving*. New York: St. Martin's Press, 1984.

Rhodes, Mary. *Small Woven Tapestries*. London: B. T. Batsford; Newton Center, MA: Charles T. Branford Company, 1973.

Tidball, Harriet. *Contemporary Tapestry*. Lansing, MI: The Shuttlecraft Guild, 1964.

Thomson, Francis Paul. *Tapestry: Mirror of History*. New York: Crown Publishers, 1980.

Verlet, Pierre et al. *The Book of Tapestry: History and Technique*. New York: The Vendome Press, 1965.

Volbach, W. Fritz. *Early Decorative Textiles*. Middlesex, England: The Hamlyn Publishing Group, 1969.

Wilson, Jean. *Jean Wilson's Soumak Workbook*. Loveland, CO: Interweave Press, 1982.

Warping Instructions

Black, Mary E. *New Key to Weaving* (13th ed.). New York: Macmillan, 1961.

Leclerc, Robert. *Warp and Weave*. L'isletville, Quebec: Nilus Leclerc, 1971.

Regensteiner, Else. *The Art of Weaving*. New York: Van Nostrand Reinhold, 1970.

Thorpe, Heather. *A Handweaver's Workbook*. New York: Macmillan, 1956.

Color Theory

Albers, Josef. *Interaction of Color*. New Haven: Yale University Press, 1963.

Birren, Faber. *Color Perception in Art*. New York: Van Nostrand Reinhold, 1976.

Ellinger, Richard G. *Color Structure and Design*. New York: Van Nostrand Reinhold, 1963.

Goethe, Johann Wolfgang. *Theory of Colours*. Cambridge, MA: The M.I.T. Press, 1970.

Guptill, Arthur L. *Color Manual for Artists*. New York: Van Nostrand Reinhold, 1962.

Itten, Johannes. *The Elements of Color*. New York: Van Nostrand Reinhold, 1970.

Lambert, Patricia et al. *Color and Fiber*. West Chester, PA: Schiffer Publishing, 1986.

Smith, Charles N. *Student Handbook of Color*. New York: Reinhold, 1965.

Design

Albers, Anni. *On Designing*. Middletown, CT: Wesleyan University Press, 1943.

Edwards, Betty. *Drawing on the Right Side of the Brain: A Course in Enhancing Creativity and Artistic Confidence*. Los Angeles: J. P. Tarcher, 1979.

Graves, Maitland. *The Art of Color and Design*. New York: McGraw-Hill, 1951.

Moorman, Theo. *Weaving As an Art Form: A Personal Statement*. New York: Van Nostrand Reinhold, 1975.

Wong, Wucius. *Principles of Two-Dimensional Design*. New York: Van Nostrand Reinhold, 1972.

Metric Conversion Chart
Inches to Centimeters

INCHES	CM.	INCHES	CM.
¼	.625	25	62.5
½	1.25	26	65
1	2.5	27	67.5
1½	3.75	28	70
2	5	29	72.5
3	7.5	30	75
4	10	31	77.5
5	12.5	32	80
6	15	33	82.5
7	17.5	34	85
8	20	35	87.5
9	22.5	36	90
10	25	37	92.5
11	27.5	38	95
12	30	39	97.5
13,	32.5	40	100
14	35	41	102.5
15	37.5	42	105
16	40	43	107.5
17	42.5	44	110
18	45	45	112.5
19	47.5	46	115
20	50	47	117.5
21	52.5	48	120
22	55	49	122.5
23	57.5	50	125
24	60		

Resources for Tapestry Weavers

Tapestry Looms

Fireside Fiberarts
625 Tyler Street
Port Townsend, WA 98368
(206) 385-7505
Gary Swett
Two-harness high-warp loom

Shannock Tapestry Looms
10402 N. W. 11th Avenue
Vancouver, WA 98685
(206) 573-7264

Paternayan Weft Yarns

Johnson Creative Arts
445 Main Street
West Townsend, MA 01474
(508) 597-8989
Three-strand Persian yarn, crewel yarn.
Write for color card.

Borg's Warp and Weft Yarns, and Unicorn Books (mail-order textile books)

Glimakra Looms 'n Yarns, Inc.
1304 Scott Street
Petaluma, CA 94954
(707) 762-3362 (queries)
(800) 289-9276 (orders)
Fiskgarn-Mattvarp warp yarn
Single and plied wool weft yarns

Tapestry Beaters and Bobbins

Woodchuck Products
324 N. Bluff
Wichita, KS 67208
(316) 684-7338
Rodney Dale Stevens

Vertical Steamer
(for blocking and steaming tapestries)

Crafts Unlimited
4986 Warwick
Memphis, TN 38117
(901) 682-2358
Evelyn Buck
The Original *jiffy* Steamer

Tapestry and Art Textile Conservation

Michelle Lester
15 West 17th Street
New York, NY 10011
(212) 989-1411

Index